MANAGING OTHERS

THE ORGANISATIONAL ESSENTIALS

THE CHECKLIST SERIES

MANAGING OTHERS
THE ORGANISATIONAL ESSENTIALS

Chartered
Management
Institute

PROFILE BOOKS

First published in Great Britain in 2013 by
Profile Books Ltd
3a Exmouth House
Pine Street
Exmouth Market
London EC1R 0JH
www.profilebooks.com

10 9 8 7 6 5 4 3 2 1

A CIP catalogue record for this book is available from the British Library.

ISBN: 978 1 78125 143 0
eISBN: 978 1 84765 974 3

Text design by sue@lambledesign.demon.co.uk

Typeset in Helvetica by MacGuru Ltd
info@macguru.org.uk

Printed and bound in Britain by Bell & Bain Ltd

The diagram on page 195 is adapted from the grief cycle model first published in *On Death and Dying* (1969) by Elisabeth Kubler-Ross. The original model has been applied here to the management of change.

All reasonable efforts have been made to obtain permission to reproduce copyright material. Any omissions or errors of attribution are unintentional and will be corrected in future printings following notification in writing to the publisher.

About the checklist series

Management can be a daunting task. Managers are expected to provide direction, foster commitment, facilitate change and achieve results through the efficient, creative and responsible deployment of people and other resources. On top of that, managers have to manage themselves and develop their own personal skills. Just keeping up is a challenge – and we cannot be experts in everything.

The checklists in this series have been developed over many years by the Chartered Management Institute (CMI) to meet this challenge by addressing the main issues that managers can expect to face during their career. Each checklist distils good practice from industry to provide a clear and straightforward overview of a specific topic or activity, and has been reviewed by CMI's Subject Matter Experts Panel to reflect new research and changes in working life.

The series is designed both for managers who need an introduction to unfamiliar topics, and for those who want to refresh their understanding of the salient points. In more specialised areas – for example, financial management – checklists can also enable the generalist manager to work more effectively with experts, or to delegate more effectively to a subordinate.

Why is the checklist format useful? Checklists provide a logical, structured framework to help professional managers deal with an increasingly complex workplace – they help shape our thoughts and save us from being confused by too much information. At the same time, checklists help us to make good use of what we already know. They help us to remember things and prevent us from forgetting something important. Thus, no matter how expert we may already be, using checklists can improve outcomes and give us the confidence to manage more effectively, and to get the job done.

About this book

Managing Others – The Organisational Essentials is aimed at anyone who manages a team within an organisation. Using a combination of action-oriented checklists and handy short summaries of the ideas of seminal thinkers on the use of power, personnel management, change management and the learning organisation, it will guide you through the basics of the Human Resources (HR) processes that a line manager needs to understand. As well as covering topics ranging from recruitment through to talent management and succession planning, this comprehensive handbook will also introduce you to the fundamentals of employee relations, including practical guidance on how to work successfully with your HR department, and show how to develop organisation policies on topics such as flexible working and email and internet use.

Contents

Introduction

To get the best out of anyone, you have to manage them well. As a line manager you have a vital role in shaping the quality of the working life of others, and can have a huge impact on the well-being and productivity of your team.

My own research over many years with the Chartered Management Institute and others has starkly demonstrated how a bureaucratic and authoritarian management style causes stress that damages the health of employees and holds back productivity and growth. Conversely, we have seen how effective management practices create high trust and healthy working environments.

Another key research finding has been the scale and impact of organisational change. Over ninety per cent of managers report recently having experienced major organisational change, compared with just a third a decade ago. Change – and heightened emphasis on cost reduction – has had a major impact: it has reduced employee loyalty and motivation as well as managers' sense of job security and of their own physical and psychological well-being.

Certainly managing an organisation in the current climate is difficult, but there are steps that all managers can take to improve matters. Accessibility, openness and good two-way communication are vitally important. As a manager, you need to get out into your organisation and talk to people in different functions and at different locations and levels. Openness and visibility breed trust and employee engagement, which in turn drive performance.

You also need to know what motivates and demotivates your team. Managers rated having the respect of their peers, autonomy and being trusted to make decisions as the most motivating ways to work. Micro-management and over-invasive performance management are the best ways to demotivate people.

Understanding the organisational context is important: how new staff are recruited, selected, promoted and rewarded; how staff are developed and trained; how the organisation makes sure that it has the talent it will need for success in future years – all these matter. You will be a more effective manager if you understand the principles underlying these processes and what impact your own behaviour can have on the bigger picture. With the right skills and knowledge you will also contribute to a happier and healthier workplace and through this to business success.

You do not need to become an expert on organisational behaviour, but you will find it much easier to do your job if you invest some time in educating yourself about the basics. Management and leadership are not easy at the best of times, and they are remarkably difficult when times are tough, but I firmly believe that by improving management practice, you can help put your organisation on the critical pathway to success.

Cary L. Cooper CBE
Distinguished Professor of Organisational Psychology and Health,
Lancaster University

Planning the recruitment process

Recruitment is the process of attracting, assessing, selecting and employing people to carry out the work activities required by a company or an organisation. This checklist focuses on planning and undertaking the initial stages of the process. This involves assessing whether there is a need for additional or replacement staff, identifying the tasks to be carried out, specifying the kind of person needed, finding a pool of suitable candidates and drawing up a shortlist.

Effective recruitment processes are crucial to ensure that an organisation has the people it needs to implement its strategy and meet its objectives. Recruitment can be expensive, but so too is the appointment of an employee who is inadequately qualified, fails to perform well or leaves the organisation before he or she has been able to make a significant contribution. The time and effort invested in planning the process of recruitment with care will help to ensure that the right person will come into the job, reducing future labour turnover and increasing competitive advantage.

Action checklist

1 Review staff requirements

Take a broad view of your staffing needs and consider whether you really have a vacancy. If an employee is leaving, review the workload and decide whether a full-time permanent replacement is needed or whether an alternative option would be more appropriate. For example, would a part-time or temporary worker be sufficient? Should the work be restructured or outsourced? What would the staffing implications of this be?

2 Consult with those involved

Take any organisational policies and procedures into account. Authorisation for a replacement or a new appointment may be needed from senior management. Consult with your personnel or HR department if you have one, as they will have expertise in this area. Ask yourself which other departments may have an interest in the appointment – it may be possible to make it a joint effort. Where possible, talk to the previous holder of the post. Discuss the job with the relevant supervisor, and especially with the people the new employee will be working with.

3 Specify the sort of person you are looking for

List the duties, responsibilities and relationships involved in the job and define the level of authority the job holder will have. If you are filling a post that has been vacated, consider whether the job should be carried out in the same way or whether there are changes that you wish to make. Decide what qualifications and skills are required, what type and length of experience are needed and which personal attributes will be important. This will enable you to draw up an up-to-date job description and person specification. State how soon the person is expected to be competent in the job and what training you are prepared to give, and set a target start date.

4 Research the labour market

Review the job description and person specification and ask yourself whether you are likely to find what you are looking for in one person. If so, undertake some research to gauge the pay and benefits package you need to offer. Salary surveys are usually expensive, but are often summarised in the press at the time of publication. Monitoring job advertisements and networking with employers in your area and sector can also give you an idea of current pay rates. You should also consider whether you will be able to find suitable candidates locally or need to look further afield.

5 Comply with legal requirements

In most countries recruitment activities are covered by legislation designed to exclude discrimination and unfair treatment. In the UK, for example, the Equality Act 2010 is designed to provide a simple and consistent framework to prevent discrimination on grounds of age, disability, gender reassignment, race, religion or belief, sex, sexual orientation, marriage and civil partnership or pregnancy and maternity. Legislation covering matters such as data protection, immigration and asylum, and the protection of children and vulnerable adults may also be relevant. Always keep yourself up-to-date with the latest legislative developments to ensure that you follow good practice and don't infringe regulations.

6 Plan how to find and attract candidates

Start by seeking potential internal candidates and considering whether there are suitable employees who could be promoted or reassigned. It is important to advertise internally as a courtesy to employees, as some people may be interested in applying, or may have friends or relatives who would be able to apply for the position.

After this:

- check your records of any previous applicants, unsolicited or otherwise, and draw on any appropriate contacts; for example, training organisations may be useful, whether you are looking for apprentices or MBAs

- decide whether to use the services of a recruitment agency to identify and shortlist candidates for you, weighing the costs incurred against the time and expertise at your disposal

- consider the use of e-recruitment sites or agencies. Many

jobseekers use online jobsites, and most organisations use online recruitment approaches to some extent, sometimes together with traditional approaches via agencies or by advertising in suitable publications.

7 Decide where to advertise

If you decide to advertise independently rather than use an agency, think about the options and decide which ones will be most likely to reach the kind of candidates you have in mind:

- local job centre
- local or national press
- specialist publications, such as the magazines of professional bodies or trade associations
- Internet recruitment sites and mailing lists.

Research the costs involved and decide what you can afford.

8 Write the advertisement

Decide whether you and/or other colleagues have the skills and knowledge required to draw up an advertisement. If your organisation has an HR or personnel department they will probably take on this task, but do ensure that you are involved throughout the process. In the case of a senior post, or if you are recruiting in large numbers, you may wish to hire an advertising agency to draft and place the advert. Use of a box number for responses will deter some applicants, so it is preferable to name your organisation in the advert, unless you have particular reasons for secrecy. Ensure that the job advert provides the following details clearly and succinctly:

- duties and responsibilities of the job
- qualifications and experience required
- personal qualities sought
- location

- some indication of the salary range
- the form of reply you require – a CV and covering letter, or completion of an application form
- deadline for the submission of applications
- whether further information is available and in what form.

It is important to ensure that the advertisement complies with relevant legislation. Bear in mind, too, that it will be on public display and ensure that it presents a positive picture of your organisation which will attract candidates.

If you are using an application form, check that it requests all the details you will need to help you assess the candidates. It can also be helpful to ask a colleague to complete the form from the perspective of a candidate to ensure that it is clear. Prepare an information pack to send out to those requesting further information.

9 Draw up a shortlist

Decide how many people you wish to interview, probably five or six at the most. Ask other colleagues, including a supervisor or manager, to help you sift through the applications and take their opinions into account. Be as objective as you can, matching the candidates against the requirements you have defined. Look out for any unexplained gaps in employment, and assess the quality of presentation and how well the replies are tailored to the specific job.

10 Reply to candidates

Contact those you do not wish to interview as quickly as possible. Treat them courteously, thanking them for their interest in your organisation and the position. You may wish to keep a few candidates in reserve, in case none of those on the shortlist proves suitable. Contact the candidates on the shortlist to check that they are still interested in the job and arrange a date and time for interview. Make sure that you provide directions so that candidates can find you, and be clear about whether you are prepared to meet travel expenses.

11 Next steps

Consider how you will organise the next steps in the recruitment process:

- carrying out the interviews, selecting the most suitable candidate and making the job offer
- organising the induction of the new recruit.

As a manager you should avoid:

- assuming there is a vacancy before reviewing the current situation carefully
- skimping on the preparation of an appropriate job description and person specification
- overlooking suitable internal candidates
- ignoring relevant legislation.

Preparing and using job descriptions

A job description is a structured and factual statement of a job function and objectives. It should also set the boundaries of the job holder's authority. The job title, department, location, a short summary of the job and key responsibilities and reporting lines are also included.

Job descriptions are still widely used, despite criticism that they are too specific and inflexible to work effectively in flatter and rapidly changing organisations. Job descriptions should be structured, however, to allow sufficient scope and flexibility to accommodate colleagues' work, needs and priorities, though not to the extent that job content becomes vague and ambiguous. Bear in mind that an organisation's work gets done through workplace relationships. How jobs are designed to fit together and how job holders work interactively matter more than spelling out the details of individual job roles. For this reason, there is a trend towards using more generic and less detailed job descriptions, which use short accountability statements focused on outcomes or key result area (KRA) statements relating to the performance measures applied to the role.

Apart from giving the job holder and immediate line manager a clear overall view of the post, job descriptions are used by HR departments to support selection and recruitment processes. Job descriptions enable recruiters to clarify the skills, experience and competencies required in a job against those of job applicants. They also give a useful basis for performance appraisal, job evaluation and job grading, and can help to identify the duplication or absence of particular functions or activities across the organisation.

Job descriptions give an overview of the purpose of a job, what it contributes to the organisation's aims and objectives, how it fits into the overall structure and, perhaps most importantly, the key tasks, responsibilities and reporting lines.

Guidance is offered here for those wishing to write a job description or update an existing one.

Action checklist

1 Inform staff of the reasons for reviewing and amending job descriptions

When existing job descriptions are reviewed, it is important to keep staff fully informed. An explanation should be given of the reasons for the review, with an assurance that job holders will be fully involved. Objectives of a job description review might be to:

- identify interdepartmental working links
- update existing job descriptions
- help with job evaluation or job grading
- give everyone a clear understanding of how the company is organised.

2 Assign responsibility

Traditionally job descriptions are prepared by the HR department and agreed with line managers and job holders. However, many organisations are devolving this responsibility to line managers, with guidance from the HR department, which checks for consistency and overlaps. The following questions should be considered:

- Are all key functions and activities listed in order of priority?
- Does each job holder have a clear reporting line?

- Is there a balance between numbers of staff and managers?
- Are there too many reporting levels?
- Are there any overlaps within departments or across the organisation?
- Are all jobs grouped logically or are some scattered?
- Are there any gaps or omissions in key functions?

3 Gather information

The person responsible for compiling the job description should consider:

- what management and the business want from the job
- what the job holder thinks he or she is doing and what they are actually doing
- what others, whose work interacts with the job holder's, think the job holder is doing and ought to be doing.

This information could be obtained from informal interviews, workgroups, or café-style meetings. It is possible to use questionnaires, but the results tend to be ambiguous, and the time required to analyse the completed questionnaires can exceed the interviewing time.

4 Put the job description together

The job description should contain the following information:

Basic information

- Job title – this should be brief, descriptive and clear. Remember that other employees will consider the status of those with the same kind of job title to be equal.
- Reporting relationships – give the job title of the person to whom the job holder reports, and job title(s) and numbers of staff reporting to the job holder.
- Location – give the location of the job, the organisation name and the department. If travel is involved this should be stated.

- Major functional relationships – where appropriate, an organisation chart will show how a job fits into the organisation and its relationship with other jobs.

Principal purpose or objective of the job

This should be a short statement describing why the job exists. For example, for a sales manager it could be simply 'ensuring that agreed sales targets are achieved'.

Key tasks/key result area statements

Key tasks and responsibilities or key result area (KRA) statements are those that make a substantial contribution towards the objectives of both the job and the organisation. These form the main part of the job and ideally there should be no more than five or six key tasks. Some basic jobs may have only one or two main activities, such as shelf-stacking and working on the checkout tills in a supermarket, though most may have several elements, such as bringing in new business, managing existing customers, managing staff, liaising with suppliers, and so on. Secondary duties and responsibilities should also be listed.

The description of each task should comprise three main components:

- a 'doing' verb to highlight the main activity, such as to develop, to design, to implement or to advise
- the object of that activity, such as stock levels, existing suppliers or a new computer system
- the central purpose of the activity, such as to reduce costs, improve efficiency or generate new income.

An example of a KRA statement incorporating these three components might be: 'To advise on the selection and implementation of a new computer system designed to forge closer links with key account customers.'

Although a job description will include outcomes, such as 'expand the existing customer base', actual target levels are not part of the job description. Targets are usually agreed separately on a regular basis – annually or half-yearly, for example – and may be incorporated into performance systems or reviews.

The key tasks or KRAs are usually listed in order of importance, or by other agreed criteria, such as chronological sequence, frequency of activity, or tasks related to a particular activity.

5 Update and review

It is wise to update job descriptions regularly, as they can quickly get out of date and cease to reflect current practice, or there may be significant changes to the job, role, or department priorities.

The job description should be examined:

- at least once a year, when the job holder is appraised
- when a job falls vacant, to ensure that the description still meets the requirements
- after a new job holder has been in post a few months, to take account of any significant changes in the job holder's duties.

As a manager you should avoid:

- restricting employee initiative through job descriptions that are too rigid
- forgetting to involve the job holder in a review of the job description
- failing to let staff know why job descriptions are being amended or updated
- letting job descriptions get out of date.

Steps in successful selection interviewing

Recruitment and selection interviews assess (or partly assess, in conjunction with other methods) an individual's suitability for a job either inside or outside their current organisation.

Job interviews are still the most popular recruitment tool, despite increasing interest in other techniques. Selecting new employees through well-designed interviewing processes will help you avoid recruiting errors and give candidates more information on your organisation. By asking the right questions in the right way in an interview you can ensure that you recruit people who will work well at your organisation, rather than those who are adept at telling you what you want to hear in interviews.

The three principal interview models are:

- biographical interviews, which explore the candidate's experiences
- structured behavioural description interviews (BDI), which seek information on how applicants behaved in past, critical incidents
- structured, situational interviews, which are based on a job analysis, with job-related questions on reactions in hypothetical situations.

The use of one technique is often preferred, but different models can be useful in different situations, and a mix of different approaches can be used if necessary. This checklist is designed to help interviewers plan, prepare and conduct interviews, whichever approach is used.

Action checklist

1 Narrow the search

Interviewing takes place at a fairly late stage in the recruitment process, and follows the drawing up of a job description, the listing of the behaviours or competencies required, the placing of advertisements and the shortlisting of candidates. The information collected from these processes will form the basis of the criteria against which candidates will be assessed.

2 Prepare for the interview

Careful planning and preparation are essential to obtain maximum benefit from the interviewing process. Some organisations prefer particular styles of interviewing, so check on policies and ensure that you adhere to them, following any necessary practices and completing the required paperwork.

● **Style.** Interviews can take many forms, such as one-to-one, sequential one-to-one, or panel. All these can be complemented by tests, presentations, group discussions and social events. Once the format has been decided upon, it is advisable to brief everyone involved, including reception staff and employees in the department where the vacancy is situated. If several people are involved in interviewing, a chair should be appointed. Decide how long each will hold the stage and what sort of questions each of them will ask.

● **Schedule.** A realistic schedule is crucial. Running late and keeping interviewees waiting for extended periods can give a bad impression of the organisation. Draw up a schedule that allows time to interview, discuss, write notes and prepare for the next person. Plan too for some breaks, as interviewing requires concentration and can prove tiring.

● **Documentation.** The application form or CV, person specification and job description are important documents to have in front of you. Read through all the relevant material beforehand, noting or highlighting particular areas of interest.

● **Environment.** Think carefully about the environment you want to create for the interview, considering your choice of room, lighting, chairs and layout, for example. Make sure drinking water is available, and in some cases it may be appropriate to have a pen and paper on the table so the interviewee can make notes. No distractions should be permitted, as they disrupt the flow of an interview and can disturb candidates. Put a notice on the door, and divert phone calls or unplug the phone. If interruptions are still possible, identify another location.

3 Inform candidates that they have been selected for interview

Inform candidates in writing as soon as possible once they have been selected for interview. Include the date and time of their interview, giving a reasonable notice period (a week may be sufficient, but with more senior posts longer notice is desirable). Decide what you will do if the candidate genuinely cannot come on the specified date. Include in the information sent:

● a location map and details of public transport and parking facilities

● the length of time the interview is likely to take

● the format of the interview (whether psychometric or aptitude tests are involved, or an assessment centre is planned, for example).

4 Work out how to record how each candidate performs

It is now common practice to use a scoring or recording method, particularly if more than one person is involved in the interview process, or if more than three or four interviews are to be held. This can bring some method into establishing, remembering and measuring the key points that will affect decisions and helps ensure that all candidates are treated fairly. Weight the criteria you have established for the post and use a systematic points rating against these for each candidate as the interview progresses.

5 Plan the questions to ask

Questions can take many forms, such as:

- **task based** – are related to a task the interviewee has been given prior to the interview and designed to reveal the interviewee's approach to getting things done

- **open** – provide an open platform for the interviewee to structure and steer the response

- **hypothetical** – allow the interviewer to establish how the candidate would act in a certain situation

- **leading** – make assumptions that the interviewee will inevitably confirm or deny

- **probing** – enable the interviewer to explore an issue more fully, and can help draw a broader picture of the candidate

- **closed** – are useful to establish precise facts, but usually lead to short 'yes' or 'no' answers

- **competency or scenario based** – require candidates to provide real life examples as the basis of their answers.

If there is more than one interviewer, plan who will ask which questions. The sequencing of questions is also important. Make sure that the first question is not too challenging, to help the candidate settle into the interview, and that the questions flow well so that there are no sudden changes of topic. Beware of asking discriminatory questions, or putting certain questions only to specific groups. Bear in mind, too, that answers to certain types of questions may be more difficult to score systematically.

6 Prepare for the interviewee's questions

Most interviewees will have questions and these may be asked throughout the interview. It is good practice to check, as the interview closes, whether there is anything further they would like to ask or add. While the interviewee is likely to ask something about the job itself or training and development opportunities, their questions could also relate to employment conditions, start date, possible help with finding temporary accommodation, or transport.

7 Set the stage

At the start of the interview it is essential to put the candidate at their ease. If there are several interviewers, the chair should introduce them all. Smile, shake hands if possible, and ask light, conversational questions to establish some rapport and create the right climate. Aim for an impassive but gently encouraging demeanour. At this point in the interview, the planned process should be explained to the candidate and further information about the role and responsibilities of the job should be given.

8 Observe closely, taking body language into account

The key to successful interviewing is to listen carefully and look deeper than the words expressed. Don't spend time thinking about how to phrase your next question (you should have decided this beforehand). While you are doing so you are not paying full attention to the candidate. Some of the following may give you an indication that something is not quite right:

- blushing
- nervous hand movements
- sudden loss of eye contact
- twitching, stammering, frowning
- any significant change in the pace of speech
- inconsistencies between words and non-verbal messages.

If you notice any of these signs, it may be worth probing more deeply on what the candidate has said. However, this could easily be caused by nervousness, in which case you should try to put the interviewee more at ease. Watch your own body language, too: make it clear to the candidate that they have your continuous full attention. Remember that the interviewee will be using the interview to judge whether they want to work for the organisation, so it is important to make a good impression.

9 Close the interview constructively

The close of an interview can be as important as the beginning. It is important to keep to your schedule by not allowing the interview to continue indefinitely. Thank the candidate for attending and explain what will happen next – whether there will be a final decision or further shortlisting, for example. Give an indication of the timescale you intend to work to – and ensure you stick to it.

10 Decide on the successful candidate

How you come to a decision can be the most difficult part of the process, particularly if interviewers disagree. Refer back to the scoring method to ensure that you base decisions on facts not feelings. If you have two candidates who are equally qualified, look for other ways of distinguishing them such as the weighting of their scores, or it may be appropriate to ask them back for a second interview or to do a presentation.

11 Practise your interviewing technique

To succeed in the role of interviewer, it is helpful to practise the necessary techniques. Test these on an experienced colleague, and if you are interviewing as a member of a panel, learn from the others and seek feedback. After each interview, review your performance and look at what you could do differently.

12 Be aware of relevant legislation

Be aware of the implications of legislation relating to data protection and equality issues. In the UK, for example, section 1 of the Employment Practices Code issued under data protection legislation covers recruitment and selection, and, in certain circumstances, gives candidates who have been rejected the right to see any notes made during or after their interview. The UK Freedom of Information Act 2000 also has implications for information requests, particularly for those interviewing within public authorities.

Interviewers will need to be acquainted with legislation covering discrimination and equal opportunities, such as the Equality Act

2010 in the UK. Organisations such as the Equality and Human Rights Commission (EHRC) and the Advisory, Conciliation and Arbitration Service (ACAS) provide guidance on recruitment for UK employers on discrimination relating to sexual orientation, religion and age.

As a manager you should avoid:

- making decisions based on a gut reaction
- departing from the schedule
- allowing interruptions
- talking too much.

Organising the induction of new recruits

Induction is the process through which a new employee is integrated into an organisation, learning about its corporate culture, policies and procedures and the specifics of the new job. Induction should not be viewed in isolation but should be treated as an extension of the selection process and the beginning of a continuing employee development programme. Rather than limited to a one-day introduction, induction should be planned and paced over several days or weeks, marking the beginning of the new employee's personal and professional development within the organisation, and allowing the employee to integrate into the organisation. In the US, induction is known as orientation.

It makes sense – for both the individuals and the organisation – to help new recruits integrate as quickly as possible into their new surroundings and become effective and proficient in their work. Failure to do so can, at the very least, lead to erratic progress, with possible hidden costs such as waste of materials and loss of customers.

A good induction will help to minimise turnover of new employees and facilitate integration and subsequent productivity.

Action checklist

1 Review the positioning of the induction

Ask yourself whether your organisational or departmental induction does the job you require it to. Ask recent recruits for their views. Does the induction process achieve its objective of familiarising new employees with the organisation and settling them into the job? Check whether the induction is the end or the beginning of their learning with your organisation.

2 Check the scope of the induction programme

Does your induction include:

- a tour of the premises showing and describing the facilities
- an explanation of the organisation chart showing where the new employee fits in
- clarification of terms and conditions and health and safety information
- exposure to, and explanation of, the organisation's culture and values, departments, products and services, and a brief organisational history
- strategic objectives and business planning for the next operational cycle
- a clear description of the job requirements?

3 Appoint a mentor

Consider asking someone on the same grade or level as the newcomer to act as a friend and adviser for the first few weeks. This will be particularly useful in a large, complex organisation or in helping to explain details not fully covered elsewhere. Take the utmost care to ensure that the mentor is the right person, with the time to do the job as you would wish.

4 Plan the induction and involve and inform others

Ideally, an induction programme should be drawn up, and certainly authorised, by the newcomer's line manager. The mentor should also be involved in the process. Others who will be working with the new employee should be made aware of the induction programme, and whether or not they will be involved. The induction plan should comprise three stages: the first day or two should cover the bare essentials; the first three or four weeks should facilitate learning through a mix of approaches; and within three to six months the newcomer should have become familiar with all departments.

Take a look at the programme and check for variety, thoroughness and a balance of learning, practising and doing. Plan too to sit through several of the sessions with the new recruit.

5 Prepare the work area

If there is a long gap between a member of staff leaving and a new employee arriving, work areas and desks can become dumping grounds for others' unwanted materials. A few days before the arrival, make sure that the work area is clear, clean and tidy. First impressions count for a lot in the welcome you intend to provide. Check that all relevant stationery and office equipment is to hand and in working order. Don't forget the little extras like an internal telephone directory and perhaps a manual on how to use the phone system.

6 Introduce the recruit to the department and the organisation

On the first day, it is usually the HR department that informs the newcomer of housekeeping arrangements (catering, for example) and covers issues contained in the staff handbook, such as salary payments, leave arrangements and the sick pay scheme. Health and safety procedures will also be high on the list as they are a legal requirement.

Make sure that the new employee has copies of any necessary documentation – the organisation chart and job description, for example. This should be accompanied by an initial but clear briefing on the structure of the chart, the role of the newcomer and the fit between the two.

The new employee must also be introduced to the department and team in which he or she will be working. Although the newcomer will be introduced to people around the organisation at this stage of the induction process, a detailed look at what other departments do should follow later.

7 Emphasise the importance of organisational policies and procedures

New employees must be made aware of policies and regulations based on legislation, particularly in the area of health and safety, at an early stage. Other procedures based on national standards, such as ISO 9001 and Investors in People, and schemes such as internal employee development or mentoring programmes, should also be introduced.

Remember that it is easy for new employees to be overloaded with information on the first day of an induction and they will not be able to absorb or remember all the details of these procedures. Build time into the induction schedule for reading, assimilation and questions, and make sure that new recruits know where to find the information they need – on the organisational intranet, or in a departmental or personal staff manual, for example.

8 Plan a balanced introduction to the work

Whether learning and development are handled by the 'sitting-with-Nellie approach' or by professional trainers, a mix of explanation, observation, practice and feedback is advisable. Beware of information overload. New employees should be given some real work to do to avoid boredom and to give early opportunities for achievement.

9 Clarify performance standards

Make the performance levels you require clear from the outset. Employees cannot be expected to meet standards of which they are unaware. Where appropriate, discuss medium- and long-term needs and opportunities.

10 Conduct regular reviews of progress

These should be made during the induction programme, for example weekly, to ensure that the employee's objectives and needs are being met. It may be necessary to adapt the programme to match individual learning requirements and speeds. Reviews will usually consist of informal chats, but a more formal appraisal interview may take place at the end of the programme, particularly if the employee is on probation. The views of the employee on the overall induction process should be sought so that the design of future programmes can be improved.

It is not always easy to foresee how long the induction process will take. However good they are, induction programmes will result in a certain amount of overload, and important questions often arise after several months in the new job. Ensure that after the official induction is over there is someone to whom the newcomer can address further questions.

As a manager you should avoid:

- forgetting that starting a new job can be a stressful experience for many
- overloading the newcomer with too much information, too much listening and too much of the same thing at any one time
- making assumptions about the recruit's learning, assimilation and integration
- enlisting the services of an inappropriate mentor
- omitting to identify training or development needs at an early stage
- failing to review the new employee's progress regularly
- sticking rigidly to the programme if experiences – or expressed needs – are showing that the recruit's needs are other than expected
- omitting an overall evaluation of the programme at the end, or when the induction moves into a new stage.

Robert Owen
Pioneer of personnel management

Introduction

Robert Owen (1771–1858) was an early industrialist, perhaps best known for his model textile factory and village at New Lanark in Scotland.

Conditions in early factories were harsh, with hazardous working conditions for all employees. Long working hours (normally at least thirteen hours a day, six days a week) were the norm, with children as young as five or six working under the same conditions as adults. Factory owners placed more importance on the care of their expensive machines than on the well-being (or otherwise) of their expendable employees. Owen's strength was that he saw his employees as every bit as important to the success of his enterprise as the machines he owned. By examining working methods and conditions, and seeking to improve these, he is justifiably claimed as a father of personnel management.

The factory owner

By the age of nineteen, Owen was joint owner of a textile factory in Manchester. Being new to the responsibilities of management, he learnt about the workings of the factory by observing his employees as they carried out their work. He wrote:

I looked very wisely at the men in their different departments, although I really knew nothing. By intensely observing everything,

I maintained order and regularity throughout the establishment, which proceeded under such circumstances much better than I had anticipated.

In 1799, Owen (with a group of partners) purchased the New Lanark mill from his father-in-law, David Dale. Even though Dale was recognised as a progressive employer, conditions in and around the factory were still poor. Children from five or six years old were employed through contracts with the local poor house, and working for fifteen hours a day was common. Owen immediately withdrew from accepting any further children from the poor house and raised the minimum age of employment to ten. He also banned the beating of children.

Although a paternalistic employer, Owen was a businessman above all else. He made no changes to employment conditions that could not be justified on economic grounds – all social improvements at New Lanark were funded through the profits of the factory. To achieve this, he required improved productivity from his workforce through changes to the working practices and methods of the factory.

For a workforce that was already working very hard, this was not popular. Owen (uniquely for the time) realised he had to gain the trust of his employees in order to get them to cooperate with the changes to the working environment he wished to achieve. He did this (in the language of today) by persuading 'champions'. He wrote:

I … sought out the individuals who had most influence among [the workforce] from their natural powers or position, and to these I took pains to explain what were my intentions for the changes I wished to effect.

Owen further won the trust of his employees when, in 1808, the US imposed a trade embargo on British goods. Most mills closed and mass unemployment occurred. Unlike other mill owners of the time, Owen kept his employees on full pay just to maintain the factory machinery in a clean, working condition.

This approach of fair management proved to be successful, and as returns from the business grew, Owen began to alter the working environment. Employment of children gradually ceased (as no further children were indentured from the poor house) and those still in employment were sent to a purpose-built school in New Lanark. The housing available to his workers was gradually improved, the environment was freed from gin shops and crime decreased. The first adult night school anywhere in the world also operated in New Lanark. Lastly, Owen set up a shop at New Lanark, and the principles behind this laid the basis for the later retail cooperative movement.

The innovator

Owen's innovations, however, did not extend merely to improving working conditions for his employees. The Industrial Revolution (which began in the mid- to late 1700s) led to a belief in the supremacy of machines. Owen opposed this growing view by seeking to humanise work. He said:

Many of you have long experiences in your manufacturing operations of the advantage of substantial, well-contrived and well-executed machinery. If, then, due care as to the state of your inanimate machines can produce such beneficial results, what may not be expected if you devote equal attention to your vital machines, which are far more wonderfully constructed.

As already indicated, Owen was one of the first to 'manage' rather than order his workforce, and the first to attempt to gain agreement for his ideas rather than impose them on others (a worker could not be sacked for disagreeing with Owen). Additionally, he required his managers to behave with some autonomy (the first example of empowerment at work?); managers (or superintendents) were selected carefully and trained to be able to act in Owen's absence.

Owen developed an aid to motivation and discipline – the 'silent monitor' system – which could be described as a distant ancestor of the appraisal schemes in use today. Each machine within the factory had a block of wood mounted on it with a different colour – black, blue, yellow or white – painted on each face. Each day the superintendents rated the work of their subordinates and awarded each a colour that was then turned to face the aisle so that everyone was able to see all ratings. The intention of this scheme was that high achievers were rewarded and slackers were motivated to improve.

The reformer

The factory at New Lanark was spectacularly profitable, with returns of over 50% on investment, and Owen held this to be proof of the validity and importance of his theories. Strengthened by his profitability, he tried to persuade other manufacturers to follow his example in employment practices. This was first attempted through those of influence who visited New Lanark (estimates put the number of visitors at an incredible 20,000 between 1815 and 1825) and then, in 1815, via his attempt to introduce a bill to legislate on working conditions in factories.

The aim of the bill was to ban the employment of those under ten, to ban night shifts for all children, to provide thirty minutes' education a day for those under eighteen, and to limit the working day to ten-and-a-half hours. This would have been enforced by a system of government factory inspectors. The bill failed to be introduced in its intended form, as its opponents argued that it would be bad for business and that in any case most employers were voluntarily doing what the bill would require. By the time it was finally introduced in 1819 the legislation was limited to banning the employment of those under nine.

In 1823, disillusioned with his failure to successfully introduce far-reaching employment legislation, but still enthusiastic about his ideals, Owen left for the US, where he founded New Harmony in Indiana. This, along with other projects, failed as a result of internal disagreements and bad planning. He returned to the UK, where in 1834 he founded (and briefly chaired) the Grand National Consolidated Trades Union and continued to push for social reform and the growth of the cooperative movement. Owen died aged 87 in 1858.

In perspective

Owen occupies a curious position in the history of management thinking. Dismissed by his contemporaries and now little recognised apart from the linking of his name with that of New Lanark, his vision and foresight place him as the pioneer of management practices which are taken for granted today.

Although many influential people visited the sites of New Lanark and New Harmony, the ideas he propounded failed to win him immediate followers. There is much debate about the reasons for this. The New Lanark factory was obviously very profitable (although as Frank Podmore argued, almost any personnel policy could have been profitable because profits in the cotton spinning industry at the time were so large), but still none of his factory-owning contemporaries adopted his ideas. Possibly the radical nature of his views contributed to this – if he had instead advocated a step-by-step approach towards improving working conditions and relations with employees instead of an 'all-or-nothing' approach, he might have been more successful.

Although it is not too surprising that resistance to his ideas came from factory owners (who may indeed have felt they had much to lose from following them), antipathy was also expressed from across the political spectrum. Some of the most long-lasting criticism was expressed by Marx and Engels in *The Communist Manifesto*. The label of 'utopian' that they applied to Owen is one by which he is still well known. The manifesto expressed the view that his ideas could not work in practice; his success at New Lanark was, they argued, due to luck rather than judgement.

Against these negative views must be set the experiences of those followers Owen did inspire. Although Owen's own partnership with Quakers and non-conformists at the end of his time at New Lanark failed (because of their wish to impose religious instruction on all), it was this sector of society that produced those who were most influenced by his ideas, including Titus Salt, George Palmer and Joseph Rowntree.

The foresight he demonstrated in areas such as motivation of employees, industrial relations and management by observation was appreciated only a century later in the work of F. W. Taylor and Mary Parker Follett, among others. In 1949, Lyndall Urwick and Edward Brech wrote of Owen:

Generations ahead of his time, he preached and practised a conception of industrial relations which is, even now, accepted in only a few of the most progressive undertakings.

Owen's lasting contribution may be best seen in the fact that for modern employers not to meet the practices he advocated is unthinkable.

Managing staff turnover and retention

Turnover refers to the percentage of employees who leave an organisation within a given period. It includes employees who leave:

- as a result of employer actions (dismissals and redundancies)
- due to dissatisfaction of varying kinds – with pay and reward, working conditions and relationships or opportunities for development and promotion, for example
- because of changes in personal circumstances (maternity leave, retirement, etc).

Retention involves managing in ways which encourage employees to remain in employment with the organisation.

All organisations need the right mix of skilled and experienced employees to achieve their aims and objectives, and employees who leave may represent a serious loss. High levels of turnover also lead to additional costs, in terms of recruitment and training costs.

It is important, therefore, for employers to be aware of the level of employee turnover in their organisation and the extent to which this may affect the organisation's ability to carry out its operations and pursue its mission. Recognise, too, that employees develop and grow during the course of their working lives – their needs and ambitions will change and so will the factors that keep them in the organisation. Failure to take account of this could have serious consequences.

Not all turnover is negative, however. New employees can contribute to the skills base and bring fresh insights and abilities into the organisation. Understanding who is leaving and why can help employers manage turnover in a positive way to ensure they have the people they need.

Effective turnover management involves assessing the amount and types of turnover that are acceptable, exploring possible reasons for turnover, and considering what you can do to retain valuable employees. It can also improve recruitment, raise morale and reduce costs.

Action checklist

1 **Establish the overall level of turnover**

Consider using one or more of the following measurement techniques.

● The global turnover rate for an organisation, otherwise known as the crude wastage index, is the most frequently used measure. It is calculated as follows:

$$\frac{\text{Leavers in year}}{\text{Average number employed in year}} \times 100$$

The advantage of this measure is that it is widely used, so comparisons can be made between companies. It has severe limitations, however, in including all leavers, and ignoring factors such as reasons for leaving, department in which the leavers worked, age and length of service. Relying on this technique may leave you with an unbalanced workforce, with, for example, all employees over fifty or under thirty.

● The stability index is a frequently used additional measure, usually calculated in this way:

$$\frac{\text{Staff with one year's service or more}}{\text{Total staff one year ago}} \times 100$$

● Cohort analysis takes a group of employees who joined at the same time and tracks the way the group behaves over a period.

The rate of leaving of this cohort can be plotted as a wastage curve.

● Census analysis takes a snapshot of the total situation, rather than examining one group over a period. Leavers are studied in groups according to length of service, and then plotted as a proportion of total staff in that group.

● Computer models for employment forecasting are used only in large firms and have become less popular.

2 Assess the extent to which turnover is problematic

Take into account that levels of turnover may vary from industry to industry and with market conditions. Turnover fluctuates with economic cycles and during a recession, for example, often falls. This may disguise underlying problems (such as dissatisfied employees or lack of new talent), so it is important to manage underlying factors relating to turnover, even though the overall level of turnover may not in itself appear to be a problem.

It is also important to consider local factors. For example, turnover in a contact centre may be higher if there is a large student population or large numbers of students in the working population. Another factor may be a high density of similar companies with similar skills requirements in the area.

3 Benchmark your organisation against others

One way of judging whether your turnover rates are reasonable is to compare them with national, regional or industry figures. Regular sources of statistics in the UK include the surveys conducted by the Confederation of British Industry (CBI) and the Chartered Institute of Personnel and Development (CIPD). Employers can also turn to periodic studies of turnover in a particular sector. Some companies belong to informal employer networks where information on various personnel topics is exchanged. If you trade turnover statistics, make sure that you are clear on other firms' definitions, so that like is compared with like.

Monitor labour market trends to assess how these will affect your organisation. These include demographic factors such as age or location; numbers of women, ethnic minorities and graduates in the workforce; and labour mobility.

4 Consider the reasons turnover takes place

External forces influencing turnover may include skills shortages in some occupational groups, but internal factors are usually more significant. The work of management theorists can provide insights into the motivation and behaviour of employees. These include:

- Victor H. Vroom, who studied the effects of employees' expectations

- Abraham Maslow, who developed the hierarchy of needs

- Frederick Herzberg, who introduced the concept of hygiene factors

- Douglas McGregor, who suggested that bosses tend to treat employees according to their own prejudices.

It is important to consider physical and hygiene factors, such as pay and working conditions, which don't promote job satisfaction but rather prevent dissatisfaction. However, other issues are just as important, and some would argue more important, in determining people's attitudes towards their work. Motivation factors vary from person to person, but may include:

- working for a good boss – bear in mind the saying that people 'join good organisations but leave bad bosses'

- having permission to think for themselves

- seeing the end result of their work and gaining a sense of achievement

- being assigned interesting and challenging work

- being informed, listened to and respected

- having their efforts recognised and appreciated

- getting opportunities for development

- working with good and supportive colleagues
- feeling valued.

It is worth bearing in mind, however, that organisations may sometimes give out conflicting messages – promoting employee engagement at a senior level, for example, while promoting a rule-driven culture on the shop floor.

5 Ask employees why they leave

It is good practice to conduct exit interviews with leavers or give them a questionnaire to complete. Whichever approach is taken, structure it carefully, and do not rely on it as the only way of collecting data. The trends behind involuntary turnover should not be ignored. For example, a rise in health-related departures may give rise to concerns about health and safety at work.

6 Assess the effects of turnover

The most obvious impact of turnover is that of increased costs. These fall into four categories:

- separation costs
- temporary replacement costs
- recruitment and selection costs
- induction and training costs.

Turnover can be self-perpetuating in that it affects the morale of those who stay. You may wish to gauge employees' reactions through the use of employee attitude surveys. Turnover also causes inefficiencies, not least because of the disruption caused by resignations.

There is a further, more intangible, aspect of turnover: that of the skills and knowledge an organisation loses when an employee leaves. Difficult to quantify and assess, this again has implications for information-sharing as well as effective motivation.

7 Implement retention strategies

Consider the following strategies:

- ensure pay rates are competitive
- offer a wider choice of benefits – for example, sabbaticals, career breaks, childcare and eldercare arrangements
- review recruitment literature to ensure it gives an accurate picture of the organisation
- improve recruitment and induction processes
- provide opportunities for learning and development
- promote career development opportunities – for example, dual career ladders for technical and managerial staff
- improve job design and consider introducing flexible working practices such as job sharing, flexitime and teleworking
- develop a culture of diversity and equal opportunity
- treat employees fairly – perceptions of unfairness will lead to disillusionment, disengagement and, potentially, resignations
- encourage meaningful two-way dialogue with employees through performance management and appraisal systems
- engage in regular communication and consultation with employees
- develop the management skills of line managers.

As a manager you should avoid:

- failing to monitor labour turnover
- being misled by global turnover rates
- spending money on retention without first exploring possible reasons for turnover
- failing to consider flexible hours and other work–life balance considerations that may encourage more employees to stay with the organisation.

Managing absence

Absence from work includes authorised and unauthorised time off. The term 'sickness absence' is generally accepted to cover all employee absences from work where ill-health or illness is given as the reason.

Absence may be authorised for a variety of reasons, such as annual leave, maternity, paternity and adoption leave, parental leave, compassionate leave and time off for public duties.

Employee absence is a matter of concern for all employers – it may disrupt workflow, cause failure to meet targets and deadlines and put additional pressure on colleagues, resulting in considerable costs to the organisation. The CBI's 2010 annual absence survey showed that the average UK employee took six-and-a-half days off in 2010 and estimated the cost of absence from work to the UK economy as £17 billion. According to the survey, while non-work-related illness and injury is by far the greatest cause of employee absence, it is also believed that 16% of working time lost is due to non-genuine sickness absence. This checklist looks at the options available to employers to manage and minimise levels of sickness absence in their organisations.

An absence policy can help to manage and reduce absence levels. It may also identify personal and organisational issues that can be addressed in order to minimise disruption, create savings and prevent unnecessary pressure being placed on co-workers. The policy should ensure that absence is tackled in a fair and consistent manner, and that, as far as possible, managerial objectivity is maintained by defining unacceptable levels of absence and the procedures to deal with them.

Action checklist

1 Ensure that you have a clear policy in place

Your policy should outline the employer's commitment to the health and well-being of their employees and explain clearly to employees what their rights and responsibilities are with regard to absence from work. The policy should include:

- notification procedures – who should be notified, and when, if an employee is unable to work; for example, employees may be required to notify either their line manager or the HR department of their absence by 10 am on the first day of absence and to give some indication of the reason for the absence and how long it is likely to last
- details of statutory and contractual sick pay arrangements
- requirements for self-certification forms and medical certificates from a doctor
- return-to-work arrangements.

2 Keep records

Research has shown that people are less likely to be absent in companies where absence is recorded, monitored and managed. Document all absences, making sure that the records comply with the provisions of data protection legislation.

3 Monitor levels of absence

Analyse patterns of short-term absence, for example by age and grade. Focus on individuals whose attendance records need special attention and evaluate trends in types of illness or accident which might indicate problems within the organisation. This will enable you to assess the extent to which you have a problem. Feed information back to line managers so that they know how effectively they are dealing with the situation. Consider encouraging managers to keep absence levels under control by publishing comparative records or league tables of the performance of different parts of the organisation. These figures will make employees aware of how much time the organisation is losing through absenteeism.

The most commonly used measure of absence is the lost time rate. This is usually calculated by the time lost due to sickness absence as a percentage of contracted working time in a defined period:

$$\frac{\text{Total absence (hours or days)}}{\substack{\text{Possible total (hours or days)} \\ \text{available in the period}}} \times 100 = \text{lost time rate}$$

For example, if the total absence in the period is 124 hours, and the possible total is 1,550 hours, the lost time rate is:

$$\frac{124}{1,550} \times 100 = 8\%$$

4 Ensure that fair procedures are followed

Approach employees who are frequently sick or have a long-term illness individually, as each case will be different. Do not deal with a person with an underlying medical condition on a disciplinary basis; take a sympathetic approach, thoroughly investigating the situation with the employee and doctors and following fair procedures. Should disciplinary action become necessary – in a case of persistent, intermittent, unconnected illness, for example – ensure that you comply with the procedures laid down by the organisational absence policy. The situation should be reviewed and discussed with the employee and, if necessary, they should be given the opportunity to improve after an informal warning that appropriate disciplinary procedures may be invoked if the situation continues.

5 Define unacceptable levels of absence

Consider setting trigger points so employees know that if they are absent more than a certain number of times within a given period, this will be investigated, for example through counselling interviews. Don't tolerate a culture where absence is accepted without explanation, where employees feel they are entitled to take a certain number of days off as sick leave or where a bad example is set by managers.

6 Be aware of relevant procedures for certifying sick leave

In the UK, employees may complete a 'self-certification' form for the first few days of absence. For employees who are off sick for longer than seven days, a system of 'sick notes' provided by doctors has been replaced by 'fit notes', which allow a doctor to provide more information on how an employee's health affects their ability to work. This is designed to help employers understand how they might be able to help employees to return to work sooner. Doctors can still say that someone is not fit for work, but in some cases they may specify aspects of jobs that workers can still perform and include comments that will help employers understand how employees are affected by a condition. Familiarise yourself with the national and organisational systems in place in your context and make sure that they are followed accurately.

7 Hold return-to-work interviews

It is good practice for line managers to meet with employees on their return to work, especially if the absence has been relatively long-term. This enables managers to reassure employees that they are valued, to ensure that they are fit to work, and to establish the reason for absence and whether it is likely to recur. If appropriate, the line manager should refer the employee to the company's doctor or occupational health service. The line manager should also take the opportunity to update the employee on developments that may have occurred during their absence. This approach will not be a problem for those who have been genuinely sick, but it can deter others from taking avoidable leave of absence. Try to find out if there are underlying causes of absenteeism such as personal difficulties or problems with motivation. Do not allow return-to-work interviews to act as substitute for daily contact with employees, however; managers should be generally aware of employees' well-being and of any problems they may be having.

8 Train your line managers

Explain to line managers why they are key figures in absence control and provide support and training for them. It is important to recognise that the policy will succeed or fail by their efforts.

9 Don't recruit poor attendees

When recruiting, ask for references that refer to the candidate's attendance record and assure yourself of their fitness for work.

10 Maintain a safe and healthy workplace

Ensure that you comply with legal requirements relating to health and safety at work. Consider encouraging healthy lifestyles by providing healthy eating options in the staff restaurant, access to exercise facilities, occupational health services and employee assistance programmes. Encourage people to take their annual leave and do not allow them to habitually work late and skip lunch. It is important, however, to consult employees about health promotion activities and not to be prescriptive.

The provision of private health insurance can speed up medical treatment in certain cases.

11 Motivate and gain commitment from staff

Motivated and committed staff are less likely to be absent, particularly in the case of minor ailments. Find out what motivates staff and influences their commitment to the organisation. Think in terms of the way they are managed, the content of their job, their role within the organisation, and their employment and working conditions. Remember that poor management can contribute

EXAMPLE RETURN TO WORK INTERVIEW FORM

Name...

Designation..

Department..

First day of absence ____/____/____

Last day of absence ____/____/____

Total number of days absent ____

Total number of days off work ____

Is absence due to an injury at work? YES/NO

Have you seen a doctor? YES/NO

Reason for absence

(Give a brief description of the illness or other reason for absence)

....

....

....

Other health issues

(Are there any other health issues that we need to be aware of before you return to work?)

....

....

....

Action taken

(Give a brief description of any action taken to date)

....

....

Proposed course of action

....

....

I understand that if I knowingly provide inaccurate or false information regarding my absence it may result in disciplinary action.

Employee's signature

....

Manager's signature

....

to high absenteeism. Ask if there are benefits that would help improve attendance, such as flexible working hours, loans for transport, or support in caring for children or elderly relatives.

12 Consider offering incentives

Consider offering attendance bonuses or rewards for good attendance. Be aware, however, of any longer-term implications that might put genuinely ill people under pressure to come to work, potentially creating additional problems. Avoid placing too much stress on the economic relationship between employer and employee to the detriment of other motivational policies.

13 Introduce return-to-work arrangements

In cases of long-term absence, it can be helpful to discuss and agree 'return-to-work' plans with employees to ease the transition back into the workplace. This may involve a gradual return, or adjustments to working hours. Where an employee has become disabled as a result of illness, the employer may, in any case, be required to make 'reasonable adjustments' to enable them to continue working, as, for example, under the UK Disability Discrimination Act 1995 and its related amendments.

14 Evaluate the absence management policy

Monitor the effects of the policy by assessing absence levels. Is the policy more successful in some areas of the organisation than others? Offer support and training to line managers as necessary.

As a manager you should avoid:

● accepting excessive absenteeism or brushing it under the carpet

● allowing an absence policy to divide staff or engender a climate of distrust.

Setting up a disciplinary procedure

A disciplinary procedure provides employers with a structured approach for taking disciplinary action against employees who fail to meet the organisation's performance standards or comply with work-related organisational policies and rules. It defines the types of unacceptable behaviour covered and the procedures to be followed for the presentation and documentation of warnings, representation at disciplinary interviews, time limits for investigations and rights of appeal

It is essential for employers to act reasonably in dealing with misconduct and ill-discipline. Following a disciplinary procedure can protect employers against claims of unfair dismissal and the costs ensuing from a successful claim. In the UK, employment tribunals will expect employers to have followed the ACAS code of practice on disciplinary and grievance procedures.

Quite apart from the legal issues, it is good people management practice to deal with all incidences of employee ill-discipline promptly and fairly, and to offer guidance on improving behaviour, so that problems do not fester and grow. A fair and thorough disciplinary procedure can help employers address behavioural problems in a consistent manner. This checklist is aimed at those wishing to implement a disciplinary procedure within their company or organisation.

Although this checklist focuses on the mechanics of a disciplinary procedure, it is important to remember that good management can prevent many cases reaching this stage, for example by spotting problems and tackling them before they become serious and by identifying development needs.

Action checklist

1 Designate those responsible for developing the procedure

This will normally be someone from the personnel or HR department, if there is one. Those overseeing the project should have project management experience, command respect, have excellent communication and negotiation skills, and be able to get things done. In larger organisations the aim should be to appoint a committee comprising at least one person from HR including a designated coordinator, one person from each level of management within the organisation, and a representative from any trade unions to which employees belong. These people will manage the design, implementation and running of the disciplinary procedure.

2 Define the terms of reference

Identify the employees covered by the procedure (for example, all non-directors) and the managers who will be responsible for disciplinary interviews. Define ill-discipline (both minor and serious misconduct), clarify legal obligations and agree on the process that could lead to dismissal. If senior managers and directors are excluded, there should be a separate process for handling any issues arising at that level.

3 Draw up the procedure

Draw on the experience of those appointed as well as soundings and research to devise the procedure. If possible, obtain samples of procedures used in other organisations. Remember to write as simply as possible so that the procedure is easy to understand and not open to misunderstanding or misinterpretation. If necessary, consider using external expertise.

The procedure should contain the following:

- **Purpose.** An initial paragraph giving the reasons for having a procedure, highlighting the benefits to employees of a consistent set of rules and the importance of discipline in the workplace.

- **Types of misconduct.** This should give employees an indication of the types of misconduct that will invoke the disciplinary procedure. Distinguish between minor offences and those which are serious or may constitute gross misconduct:

Minor	Serious
• Smoking (where appropriate)	• Vandalism
• Timekeeping	• Fraud
• Misuse of company facilities	• Alcohol, drugs
• Dress	• Violence, bullying

- **Warnings.** Depending on the seriousness of the offence an employee will be faced with a series of warnings:
  - oral (confirmed in writing)
  - written
  - final written.

  The ultimate penalty after this will be dismissal, although sanctions short of dismissal such as transfer, demotion or loss of pay may be considered.

  The warnings will be given to the employee after an interview, usually with the employee's line manager. Many procedures stipulate a length of time after which, if the employee does not reoffend, the warning lapses, but this can leave the door open to abuse of the system. For this reason it is best not to set a time limit, and to keep the warning on file. Remember that the disciplinary procedure should not be invoked unless informal warnings from the line manager have had no effect, or the offence is considered to be so serious that instant disciplinary action must be taken. In cases of gross misconduct, an employee may be suspended from work, on full pay, pending an investigation and then dismissed.

- **Representation at meetings.** A colleague or trade union representative can, by right, accompany or represent the employee at each warning interview. Consider stipulating that the union should be involved unless the employee specifically objects. On occasions when the offence also constitutes a criminal offence, a solicitor should be allowed to be present.

- **Investigations.** All abuses of discipline must be investigated before a warning of any kind is issued. At the very least this involves hearing the employee's side of the story. It is possible to suspend the employee on full pay while the investigation is taking place. Set a time limit to carry out investigations into gross misconduct, such as deliberate malpractice. This should be not more than ten days after the offence was reported.

- **Documentation.** Detailed minutes should be taken at all interviews and kept along with copies of any investigation into the misconduct and any warnings issued. Consider designating a separate person to take notes or making an audio recording of the interview. This documentation is not only useful for checking whether an employee's behaviour improves; it can also be used as evidence, in the event of an employment tribunal, that correct procedures have been followed.

- **Plans of action.** In the case of minor offences every effort must be made to help the employee overcome problems, obviating the need to take the process further. The procedure should make it clear that plans of action will be agreed between the employee and the line manager at each interview to enable improvements in discipline. A date will be given for an evaluation interview, at which, if progress has not been made, a more severe warning can be issued.

- **Appeals.** Employees should be given the right to appeal against any warning they receive, as long as it is made in writing to their line manager within five working days of the issue of the warning.

4 Draw up an implementation timetable

In a large organisation it is often better to pilot the disciplinary procedure on one site or in a large department before full implementation.

5 Provide training for managers and supervisors

Training should be given to all managers and supervisors who may have to deal with disciplinary issues. Ensure that they understand the mechanics of the procedure and try to make sure that there is a consistency of approach. Give training not only in conducting a disciplinary interview effectively but also on general discipline and control; this will help solve as many problems as possible without the need for the full procedure. Repeat this training for new managers and consider refresher training for those who are not frequently involved in disciplinary matters.

6 Communicate the procedure to all employees

If you have disciplinary rules, by law they must be notified to employees. Ensure that staff are aware of the procedure (a letter should be sent to all employees along with a copy of the procedure) and know when it will come into effect. Explain that the procedure has been introduced to benefit employees by providing them with a consistent way of dealing with ill-discipline. The same information should be given to new recruits and included in the staff manual or organisational intranet.

7 Implement the procedure

Ensure that an appropriate person is available to answer any questions that may arise, especially during the critical period following the communication of the procedure.

8 Evaluate the procedure

Regular evaluation of the procedure will contribute towards improving it. The number of times the procedure is used should be recorded, and any managers who seem to have difficulty in handling discipline should be identified, so that additional support and/or training can be provided. Employees who have been disciplined under the procedure should be asked for their views on it.

9 Make changes and give feedback on the results

Changes should be made in the light of the evaluation. These may include extra training for some managers, or rewriting some of the steps or phases. Notify employees of any changes.

As a manager you should avoid:

● taking disciplinary action until the case has been investigated

● setting the procedure in stone by ignoring the need for regular reviews

● making the assumption that the procedure can replace the need for good management.

Mary Parker Follett
Prophet of management

Introduction

Mary Parker Follett (1868–1933) was one of the first people to apply psychological insight and social science findings to the study of industrial organisation. She is recognised by many well-known management theorists, including Peter Drucker, Rosabeth Moss Kanter and Henry Mintzberg, as a great management philosopher.

Follett's work focused on human relations within industrial groups, and many businessmen became convinced of the practical applications of her ideas. She, in turn, viewed business as a vital, exciting and pioneering field within which solutions to human relations problems were being tested out, to the ultimate benefit of the rest of society.

After the Second World War, Follett's name became less known and her ideas were largely neglected, except in Japan where they had a formative influence on management culture and practice. Yet her work foreshadowed, and often preceded, current Western approaches emphasising involvement and cross-functional communications. More recent interest in Follett since the 1960s owes much to Pauline Graham, a management consultant and writer, who has worked hard to reclaim and disseminate Follett's work.

Background

Born in Massachusetts to a well-off Boston family, Follett was a brilliant scholar who graduated at the age of twelve. She was educated at the Thayer Academy, Boston, and Radcliffe College, Massachusetts. At twenty she attended an annexe of Harvard University called the Society for Collegiate Instruction of Women. In 1890, as a student of twenty-two, she spent a year at Newnham College in Cambridge, UK, and went on to Paris as a postgraduate student. Graham describes Follett as a polymath, and records that she read law, economics, government and philosophy at Harvard, and history and political science at Newnham.

While at Cambridge, Follett gave a paper which she later developed into her first book, *The House of Representatives*. This was taken seriously enough to be reviewed by Theodore Roosevelt in the *American Historical Review* in October 1896.

Follett's family life was difficult. Her father, to whom she was close, died when she was in her early teens. Her mother was an invalid with whom Follett did not get on very well. From an early age Follett ran the household, and later she also ran the family housing business. Eventually, Follett broke all family ties and went to share a home with a friend, Isobel Briggs. Over the next thirty years, Briggs provided a stable domestic background, while her social connections were helpful to Follett's work. When Briggs died in 1926, Follett lost her home life as well as her closest friend.

Later that year she met Dame Katherine Furse, an English woman who was strongly involved with the Girl Guide movement. Follett later moved to the UK to share a house in Chelsea with Furse.

The social worker

Follett was expected to become an academic, but instead she went into voluntary social work in Boston, where her energy and practicality (as well as her financial support on occasions) achieved much in terms of community-building initiatives. For over thirty years she was immersed in this work, and proved to be an innovative, hands-on manager whose practical achievements included the original use of schools as out-of-hours centres for community education and recreation. This was Follett's own idea, and the resulting community centres became models for other cities throughout the US.

Follett set up vocational placement centres in Boston school centres, and represented the public on the Massachusetts Minimum Wage Board. From 1924, she began to give regular papers relating to industrial organisation, especially for conferences of the Bureau of Personnel Administration in New York. She became, in effect, an early management consultant, as businessmen began to seek her advice about their organisational and human relations problems.

In 1926 and 1928, Follett gave papers for the Rowntree Lecture Conference and the National Institute of Industrial Psychology. In 1933, she gave an inaugural series of lectures for the new-founded Department of Business Administration (now the Department of Industrial Relations) at the London School of Economics (LSE). Later in 1933, Follett returned to the US, where she died on 18 December of that year, aged 65.

Key texts

The New State was written during 1918 and argues for group-based democracy as a process of government. Through this book, Follett became widely recognised as a political philosopher. It was based on her social work experience rather than on business organisation, but the ideas it contains were later applied in the business context.

The New State presented an often visionary interpretation of what Follett viewed as a progress of social evolution, and the tone is occasionally infused with religious poesy. The book argues that democracy 'by numbers' should give way to a more valid process of group-based democracy. This form of democracy is described as a dynamic process through which individual conflicts and differences become integrated within the search for overall group agreement. Through it, people will grow and learn as they adapt to one another's views while seeking a common, long-term good.

The group process works through the relating of individuals' different ideas to each other and to the common interests of the group as a whole. Appropriate action would, Follett held, become self-evident during the consultation process. This would eventually reveal a 'law of the situation', representing an objective which all could see would be the best course for the group as a whole to pursue. Conflict or disagreement were viewed as positive forces, and Follett considered social evolution to progress through the ever-continuous integration of diverse viewpoints and opinions in pursuit of the common good.

The New State envisages the basic group democratic process following right through to the international level, feeding up from neighbourhoods via municipal and state government levels into the League of Nations. Sometimes, Follett refers to an almost autonomous group spirit, which develops from the community between people, as the group process begins to work.

The Creative Experience was also written during 1918, and again focused on democratic governance, using examples from business to illustrate ideas. *Dynamic Management: The Collected Papers of Mary Parker Follett* and *Freedom and Co-ordination* were both published posthumously and edited by L. Urwick. *Freedom and Co-ordination* collects together six papers given by Follett at the LSE in 1933, and these represent the most developed and concise distillation of her thoughts on business organisation.

Follett's business writings extended her social ideas into the industrial sphere. Industrial managers, she saw, confronted the same difficulties as public administrators in terms of control, power, participation and conflict. Her later writings focused on management from a human perspective, using the new approach of psychology to deal with problems between individuals and within groups. She encouraged businessmen to look at how groups formed and how employee commitment and motivation could be encouraged. The participation of everyone involved in decisions affecting their activities is seen as fundamental, in that Follett viewed group power and management through cooperation as the obvious route to achievements that would benefit all.

Power, leadership, authority and control

Follett envisioned management responsibility as being diffused throughout a business rather than wholly concentrated at the hierarchical apex. Degrees of authority and responsibility are seen as spread all along the line. For example, a truck driver can act with more authority than the business owner in terms of knowing most about the best order in which to make his drops. Leadership skills are required of many people rather than just one person, and final authority, while it does exist, should not be over-emphasised. The chief executive's role lies in coordinating the scattered authorities and varied responsibilities that make up the organisation into group action and ideas, and also in foreseeing and meeting the next situation.

Follett's concept of leadership as the ability to develop and integrate group ideas, using 'power with' rather than 'power over' people, is very modern. She understood that the crude exercise of authority based on subordination is hurtful to human beings, and cannot be the basis of effective, motivational management control. The power of single individuals, Follett considered, could erode overall organisational and social achievement, and she advocated the replacement of personal power with the authority of task or function and with the 'law of the situation', as revealed through group process consultation. Partnership and cooperation, she sought to persuade people, was ultimately of far more benefit to everyone than hierarchical control and competition.

Follett viewed the group process as a form of collective control, with the interweaving experience of all who are performing a functional part in an activity feeding into decision-making. Thus control is realised through the coordination of all functions rather than imposed from the outside.

Four fundamental principles of organisation

Follett identified four principles that she considered basic to effective management coordination:

- Coordination as the 'reciprocal relating' of all factors in a situation – relating the factors in a situation.

- Coordination by direct contact – direct communication between all responsible people involved, whatever their hierarchical or departmental positions.

- Coordination in the early stages – involving all the people directly concerned, right from the initial stages of designing a project or forming a policy.

- Coordination as a continuing process – keeping coordination going on a continuous basis, and recognising that there is no such thing as unity, but only the continuous process of unifying.

In perspective

Follett's thinking was ahead of her time, yet was founded on a conviction of social, evolutionary progress, which, from our hindsight perspective, is flawed by the course of subsequent history. She lived through momentous times, when social and technological change seemed to make a new order inevitable. The destruction caused by the First World War also seemed to dictate the clear need for a determined effort to create a social order which would not break down so disastrously. Simultaneously, the war created pressures in the UK and the US to include labour participation in management, and led to a growth in internationalist ideas and to the birth of the League of Nations. Like other writers of the time, Follett made leaps of the imagination that grew out of the changes that were actually taking place. Her view was rational and progressive, and she could not know the degree to which some things would remain constant, undermining the apparently inevitable dynamic of social 'progress'.

At the end of the same century which Follett saw begin, we had only too full a knowledge of the Second World War and countless other conflicts, of the discrediting of Russian communism, and of worsening ethnic divisions and continuing human barbarities. The progressive, internationalist vision seems to be, from our contemporary perspective, a fast-receding dream.

Yet while Follett's optimistic expectations of radical social change were largely mistaken, she drew from them the imaginative vision to transform at least some of her convictions into ideas about ways of living and working that have contributed much to both social and management practice. In fact, it is almost disheartening to read Follett and realise that she clearly and strongly stated, so many years ago, ideas that are being proffered as 'new' today and that are still rarely practised in any sustained way.

Managing a secondment

Secondment is the temporary loan or attachment of an employee either to another organisation or to a different department or section of the same organisation, for a specific purpose, for a defined length of time and for the benefit of all concerned.

Secondments are often used as mid-career development opportunities, offering value to all parties. They are not generally sponsored, although they may be subsidised by the seconding organisation. For this reason, everyone needs to be clear about the objectives and expected outcomes of a secondment. Secondments may last anything from one week to three years, but there is a growing trend towards shorter attachments. Short or part-time secondments focusing on specific projects can provide good value; longer secondments cost more but allow more time for the maximum benefits to be gained.

Secondments can give host organisations or departments access to expertise that they might not otherwise be able to afford, as well as providing additional labour for specific projects and bringing a fresh perspective to the project. For employers, secondments may create excellent public relations opportunities, and for the people seconded, they offer valuable experience that will support their personal and career development.

In this checklist the employee to be seconded is referred to as the secondee, the supplying organisation is called the employer, and the receiving organisation is called the host. This checklist is intended primarily for managers in small, medium-sized or voluntary organisations that are considering hosting a secondee and want to get the best from those who are seconded to their organisation.

Action checklist

1 Decide whether a secondment is appropriate

Consider why you need a secondee and evaluate the nature of the work you have in mind. Is there a shortage of skills within a particular business area or location? Do you have a particular project to progress? Do you want to fill a key role by a means other than recruiting a permanent employee? What can you offer? For example, can you offer high-level networking, political exposure, or financial experience? What advantages are there to encourage individuals to take part, and employers to release them? Write a person specification identifying the skills needed by the secondee (for example, communications abilities, budgetary experience, or good interpersonal skills). Establish what resources may be required to support the secondee and the most appropriate person to manage the secondment.

2 Identify suitable organisations to approach

Find out which employers might have an interest in your project or business because of shared or related aims, or a wish to help the local community. Find out more about employers' secondment policies. Recognise that the employer will incur financial costs by agreeing to a secondment, as they will probably have to cover the secondee's post, and that they may have reservations about passing on expertise to another organisation. Personal contacts are often more effective than formal requests. In some cases it may be appropriate to approach an organisation involved in coordinating secondments between business and voluntary organisations or business and government.

3 Decide on the objectives of the secondment

Work with the employing organisation to establish the boundaries of the project and its objectives. Establish what benefits are to be gained by all three parties: your company as host, the secondee and the employer. Write a specific job description setting out:

- background information on the organisation and the assignment
- the type and length of the secondment
- the role and responsibilities of the secondee
- special circumstances or conditions peculiar to the secondment
- the line manager for the secondee
- the host's link with the employer.

4 Clarify terms and conditions of employment

Be aware that legally the secondee's employment rights rest with their original employer. It is wise therefore for both the HR department in the host organisation and a manager at the employing organisation to keep in touch with a secondee so that any mismatch in rights or any problems that arise can be handled effectively. Establish whether the employer will continue to pay the secondee's salary, and agree any changes in terms and conditions which will apply during the secondment, such as hours of work, overtime, holidays and payment of expenses. Consider any implications for security of employment, pension rights or benefits, and set down the full terms and conditions of the secondment in writing for all three parties. A formal contract may be required, and in any case a probationary period should be incorporated into any agreement to protect all parties.

5 Meet the secondee

Suggest that you are involved in the selection process, but if this is not possible insist on meeting the proposed secondee. Find out how they (and their employer) view secondment: for example, is it seen as a promotion or a sideways move? Make sure they are enthusiastic and committed and not under any pressure to agree to the assignment. Check that they understand the aims of the project, and are self-motivated and capable of adapting quickly to new situations and people. Ensure that they are available for the time required, and, if possible, encourage them to speak to others who have been on secondment. Clarify return arrangements for the benefit of all parties. The return should be at an appropriate level, or the individual may become demotivated both during and after the secondment.

6 Help the secondee to settle in

Remember that the working conditions and culture in your organisation may be very different from what the secondee is used to. Run an induction programme to help with the familiarisation process, bearing in mind that the secondee is neither simply an employee nor simply a guest, but both. Where secondees are managing other employees, they must receive the same level of information (staff handbooks, memos, access to staff files) as other managers.

7 Ensure that the secondee maintains contact with their own organisation

Suggest that the employer appoints a contact person to offer support and advice to the secondee. Such an arrangement can help the secondee resolve conflicts of interest that may occur. It can also keep the employer in touch with the skills being developed, so that best use can be made of them on the secondee's return. Some employers provide their secondees with the names of other secondees they are sponsoring, to give an extra level of support. Encourage the employer to continue to invite the secondee to meetings and social functions and to send out newsletters or email circulars so that the secondee can keep in touch.

8 Monitor performance and results

Responsibility for appraisal may rest with the host organisation. Agree an appropriate method with the employer for measuring the success of the secondment for all parties concerned. Undertake regular review meetings attended by the host, employer and secondee, the frequency of which will be determined by factors such as perceived need, the nature of the role, or the seniority of the employee. Encourage the secondee to keep a log, and make it a condition that the secondee writes a report (available to both host and employer) at the end of the secondment.

As a manager you should avoid:

- allowing the secondee to lose contact with their employer
- neglecting to arrange satisfactory return arrangements for the secondee
- using the secondee as just another pair of hands
- forgetting to give an appropriate induction
- making the secondment period too long.

Managing part-time employees

Part-time work is when employees are contracted to work for anything less than the normal basic full-time hours. There is no specific number of hours indicating full-time or part-time work, but in many employer surveys people are classified as part-time if they work thirty hours or less in a week, and full-time if they work more than thirty hours a week.

ACAS has reported that in the UK, part-time employees make up 25% of workers and 80% of them are women. Part-time working is becoming more common at all levels within organisations, and increasingly companies rely upon part-time employees to achieve flexibility in running their businesses, to respond to changes in demand, or in helping to deliver round-the-clock services.

Part-time employees need to be managed in the same way as their full-time equivalents. In the UK, they have the same employment rights and may not be treated less favourably than full-time employees. Less favourable treatment could risk a complaint to an employment tribunal, or lead to a claim of indirect sex discrimination (as the majority of part-time employees are women), or reduce their effectiveness as valued employees within the organisation.

There is a perception that managing part-time employees involves extra management time and employment costs. Though this may be true in some cases, the benefits to be gained from employing part-time employees outweigh the potential difficulties of managing them. These include increased flexibility in managing workloads and supporting operational requirements. Retention of valued employees and improved employee commitment are also important benefits. Considering a wider range of positions for part-time working widens recruitment opportunities. Absenteeism, too, can often be reduced when part-time working is introduced. The most common problems related to part-time working occur when trying to arrange meetings and organise training and development.

Action checklist

1 Induction

Plan induction programmes for part-time employees that make them feel respected, valued and part of the team. It is important to make new members of staff feel welcome and to introduce them to the business and their role. Spending time on the induction of new employees will save time and problems in the long run. Your expectations of their performance and how their progress will be measured should be discussed at the induction stage.

2 Work allocation

It can be tempting to assign all low-level work to part-timers; however, overloading them with routine tasks can be demoralising. Consider assigning projects rather than several unrelated tasks, or giving them opportunities for job rotation. As there may be less opportunity to meet with part-timers as the project proceeds, be specific about the direction you want the project to go in.

3 Rewards and recognition

Part-time employees deserve their fair share of credit for work well done, so don't single out only full-time staff for rewards and recognition. Remember that every employee is critical to the success of the organisation.

4 Benefits available to part-time employees

It is good practice for employers to offer the same benefits pro rata as those given to full-time staff unless an objective justification for not doing so can be made. In the UK this is required and applies to:

- pension schemes
- health insurance
- training
- holiday entitlement pro rata as comparable full-timers
- profit sharing and share option schemes
- being selected for redundancy
- contractual maternity and parental leave
- staff discounts.

Employers can decide to withhold benefits from part-time employees on the grounds that costs would be prohibitive. However, it is not enough to show that a benefit could not be applied pro rata; it must also be shown that the decision is justified on objective grounds. A way must be found to apply benefits that cannot be applied pro rata to part-time employees, such as by calculating the financial value of the benefit to a full-time employee and then applying that value pro rata to a part-time employee.

5 Access to training and development

Access to training is essential if part-time employees are to work effectively and they should not be excluded from training because of their employment status. Denying or excluding part-time employees from access to training would obviously constitute less favourable treatment and employers should consider all applications for training and career development on their merits. Consider:

- organising training in a way that is convenient for part-time employees

- paying part-time employees (at their normal rate of pay) for the extra hours they attend outside their normal working hours
- offering an equivalent course at a convenient time and place
- offering an equal level and quality of training in another area or other training methods, such as open or distance learning or e-learning courses.

6 Communication

Effective communication is an essential skill in managing part-time employees successfully. Part-timers need to be kept as well informed as their full-time equivalents. Communication can be a problem, however, as part-time employees can be overlooked or treated as invisible because they are not always around. Managers should consider regular one-to-one meetings with all staff including part-timers. Knowing in advance what you want to discuss will pay dividends. Part-time employees are more likely to miss changes in priorities or important nuances of company culture that can affect how things get done. Regularly check your assumptions about how well part-timers understand priorities, organisational objectives and their own jobs. Ask them what they want and need to be more productive members of the team. Effective internal communications, in the form of emails, newsletters, intranets and notice boards, will help part-time employees, in particular, keep abreast of events.

7 Feedback

Feedback is not just an issue for full-time employees, and whether the feedback is positive or negative, constructive criticism or praise is as necessary for part-timers as for full-timers. Feedback can facilitate the communication process between managers and part-timers, leading to more positive relationships, and is a means of keeping up-to-date on performance issues.

8 Rotas

If possible, plan the rotas for part-time employees several weeks in advance. Have a rota posted so that you and other members of the team know who is supposed to be where and when.

9 Motivating part-time employees

Part-time employees can present a special challenge when it comes to motivation as they often carry out more routine work, tend to have fewer career choices and may be focused on other goals outside the organisation. To find out what motivates them, you can ask questions such as 'What do you want to do in the future?'. You can then relate their future goals to your present needs. Through asking questions such as this you may also find that part-timers have talents that are useful to the organisation.

10 Employer responses to requests to increase or decrease hours

Changes in working hours are a contractual matter and must be agreed with the employees concerned, although in the UK some groups such as parents of young children have the right to request (but not to insist on) flexible working. Employers should consider carefully whether there is a good business reason for refusing requests for part-time working, and requests from both men and women to change hours should be treated in the same way. Thought should be given to the circumstances of individual employees, and as much notice as possible should be given. Employers should also aim to maximise the range of posts designated as suitable for part-time working.

As a manager you should avoid:

- failing to communicate with part-time employees – they need to be kept as informed as their full-time equivalents; failure to communicate effectively can mean that part-timers are not kept up-to-date with developments in the workplace

- failing to recognise their contribution or to accept that part-time employees want to feel challenged in their work, share ideas and be valued equally with full-time workers; failure to do this may undermine the confidence of part-time employees

- ignoring the training and development needs of part-time employees – they have the same training needs as full-time employees, relative to the hours they work

- forgetting the constraints that part-time employees may be under – try to be flexible in allowing individuals to change their hours in the event of a change of circumstances at home

- excluding part-time employees from opportunities to develop their skills by varying their tasks – this means that you may not get the best results from them.

Mapping human resource skills

A skill is the ability to perform a task proficiently. In the context of this checklist, the mapping of human resource skills is understood as investigating and recording a considered and defined range of employees' work-related skills and qualifications.

The mapping of human resource skills is a complex, demanding and bureaucratic activity, and some experts consider skills mapping to be of low practical value. Others find it extremely worthwhile, however, whether they map people's skills and talents on an informal, networking basis, or set up more formal programmes to do it. Where formal programmes are used, they are likely to be part of a broader knowledge or information management strategy, which aims to identify, and record, specific aspects of employees' work knowledge, talents and skills.

Mapping schemes can extend to identifying skills employees use outside their work, but managers should be cautious about this, and specifically identify any externally used skills that they want to attempt to map.

If applied with sensitivity and selectivity, within a well-planned programme that is maintained with care, human resource skills mapping can enable managers to:

- save money by using identified in-house skills
- produce plans that make more use of employees' skills and abilities

- identify any skills gaps or areas of strength and weakness within the organisation

- enhance the feel-good factor by demonstrating interest in employees as 'whole' individuals

- motivate employees, especially those who want to use their skills for the benefit of the organisation.

Action checklist

1 Obtain management backing

The time and resources needed to collect and analyse information on the skills of employees will be considerable, so estimate the costs, and ensure that you have the commitment of senior management to the project. It will need to be coordinated by a manager with project management experience who commands enough respect to get things done.

2 Define the terms of reference

Define what types of skill and areas of experience should be recorded and (unless you plan to include the skills of all) identify employees who will be covered by the system. Information collected might include formal qualifications, foreign language skills, or experience of setting up and installing an IT system or implementing a quality scheme.

Skills involved in effective management could include time management, prioritising, teamworking or teambuilding, networking, project management, planning, coaching, influencing, exercising judgement, strategic thinking, analytic skills, mastering stress, or similar abilities. Softer, interpersonal skills are extremely important for managers, but they involve subjective judgements that are difficult to substantiate. Harder skills, which involve managing resources rather than people, are easier to judge objectively and measure.

3 Assign responsibility

One person should be given responsibility for the collection of skills data from each section or department in the organisation, and for keeping the skills system up-to-date in their area.

4 Formulate a data collection method

Three methods are available for direct collection of skills data:

- **questionnaires** – while difficult to design and sometimes inadequately filled in by respondents, questionnaires to each employee are a relatively inexpensive way to collect data

- **interviews** – these are more time-consuming than questionnaires (though they usually gather more information) and someone would be needed to interview each employee

- **a combination of questionnaires and interviews** – in the case of a combined approach, employees would complete an initial questionnaire, with an interview follow-up as necessary.

All these methods involve employee self-reporting, and most people will inevitably report themselves in a favourable light. To be certain about the reliability of the information, therefore, the inclusion of some 360 degree feedback input from supervisors, colleagues and other work contacts is advisable.

5 Train staff in data collection

Train assigned staff to collect skills data, on the types of skills to include and on how to input the data into the system. If interviews are planned, practice interviews are a useful training exercise. The provision of guidelines will give some structure and consistency to gaining information on relevant skills.

6 Pay close attention to privacy and data protection legislation

Be sure to comply with the relevant data protection legislation in your country. In the UK most organisations are required to register with the Information Commissioner and provide information on:

- personal data held by the data user and the purposes for holding it
- sources from which the data was obtained
- people to whom the data may be disclosed and countries to which it may be transferred.

The UK Data Protection Act also requires that registered data users comply with data protection principles stating that personal information shall be:

- collected fairly and lawfully and kept secure
- used only for the purposes stated in the register
- adequate, relevant and not excessive to the purposes stated
- accurate, up-to-date and not held for longer than necessary
- accessible to the individuals concerned who, where appropriate, can have information about themselves corrected or erased
- transferred to countries outside the European Economic Area only if there is adequate protection.

Individuals can seek compensation through the courts if damage is caused by the loss, destruction, inaccuracy or unauthorised disclosure of personal data held by a data user.

7 Communicate the system to all employees

Communicate the advantages of the scheme to all whose skills will be registered. Benefits can include:

- greater utilisation of an employee's skills, leading to greater job satisfaction
- more varied work, as employees from different departments are pulled into cross-functional teams
- a general increase in internal promotions if suitable in-house candidates can be found more easily.

Successful promotion of the scheme will encourage employees to take part and to volunteer information when they acquire new skills. It is important, however, to take account of the psychological impact of a skills database on those who are lower-skilled or more fearful by nature, as the motivational costs are sometimes underestimated. Some people are motivated by the possibilities of promotion or distinction, but others can feel threatened or fear being exposed as, perhaps, easily replaceable or too inexperienced.

8 Implement the scheme

Stage 1: let employees know who will be collecting skills data in their department or on their site, how the data will be collected, and who they can contact with any questions or issues regarding the scheme.

Stage 2: collect and input the data.

Stage 3: promote the system within the organisation and make sure it is used, for example to fill a new post in-house or to put together appropriate project teams.

9 Evaluate the success of the system

Seek feedback on how useful the skills data has been for users, and broadcast successes by, for example, publicising the results internally. Monitor any problems or complaints and modify the scheme as necessary.

10 Keep the system up-to-date

Update the system regularly, at least once a year, as a list of outdated skills will not prove useful. Always remove details of individuals who leave and add the skills of new employees who join the organisation.

As a manager you should avoid:

- failing to carefully consider and define the skills you wish to identify
- forgetting that the information held on the database must be secure
- loading the scheme with political or performance measurement overtones.

Implementing a job evaluation scheme

Job evaluation is a system for analysing and comparing different jobs and ranking them according to the overall demands of each one. It aims to provide a systematic, rational and consistent approach to define the relative worth of jobs within an organisation.

This checklist offers guidance on implementing a job evaluation scheme. It does not explain in detail the various approaches to job evaluation.

Job evaluation is not concerned with the volume of work, with the person doing it, or with determining pay rates. It is used to provide the basis for a fair and justifiable pay structure, particularly in determining equal pay for equal value.

Job evaluation schemes can be divided into two main categories: non-analytical and analytical. The non-analytical method takes one job as the benchmark against which all others are assessed; certain factors in a job are examined in comparison with the benchmark. Another method is to define a grading structure first, then review job specifications within that framework and make any adjustments.

In an analytical scheme a job is split up into a number of different aspects and each factor is measured separately. Each job will be assessed on a number of factors, such as the size of the budget controlled, the number of staff reporting to the post, direct interface with customers, the level of technical expertise required and the potential impact on the organisation's success.

Points are awarded for each factor from a predetermined set of specifications (for example, 5 points if there are 4 or fewer staff reporting, 12 points if there are 5–15 staff, 20 points if there are 16–50 staff, and so on) and the total reached indicates the final level of importance. This is then reviewed to take account of any further issues that have an impact on the job's value. The main types of analytical schemes are factor comparison, point-factor rating, competency-based schemes and the profile method.

Job evaluation aims to:

- establish a fair and workable system of differentials between various jobs in the organisation
- sort out anomalies between similar jobs in different parts of the same organisation
- review how the jobs in an organisation have changed over time
- assess the value of a job that is hard to fill
- provide a relatively objective, unbiased view of the worth of jobs
- avoid favouritism or patronage
- iron out current discrepancies and help to prevent future anomalies
- provide a transparent approach to valuing jobs once established.

The job evaluation process can be lengthy and costly to plan, introduce and implement, especially if an analytical approach is taken and an external consultancy is used. There can be an emotional backlash if a job evaluation scheme is introduced without adequate consultation and communication. Schemes require adequate representation from all grades and specialisms – individuals should have no grounds for complaint in terms of feeling misunderstood or remote.

Job evaluation is a specialised process usually handled by HR specialists. Line managers, however, have a large role to play in helping to define jobs and in implementing the results.

Action checklist

1 Carry out some background research

Before starting, it is crucial to think through the implications, make sure that job evaluation is the route you wish to follow and, if so, decide whether you are going to adopt an analytical or a non-analytical approach. You need to:

- decide what you want a job evaluation scheme to achieve
- keep an open mind, as it may bring other issues to light
- consider whether there is an easier, more direct way of tackling the issue that might be adequate
- try to find one or more colleagues in other organisations with experience of the process.

If you are planning to use a detailed, analytical approach, research it thoroughly. Talk to consultants and read up on it – this is not a route to be followed lightly. Once you have all the information, carry out a detailed cost–benefit analysis to identify whether the costs of undertaking job evaluation are outweighed by the benefits.

If you judge that the benefits of using a job evaluation scheme are significantly greater than the costs, move on to the next part of the checklist. If not, look for more appropriate ways of achieving your objectives.

2 Decide on the approach

On the basis of the cost–benefit analysis, decide whether to bring in a consultant and use an analytical process, or to do what you can on your own on a less complex basis.

Having chosen the approach, plan your steps carefully and consider all the essential details, such as:

- whether job descriptions, as they form a major element of job evaluation, are all up-to-date, or whether work will be needed to amend them

- who will be managing the process in-house, either as the prime mover or as the contact point for an external consultant
- how much time you need to allow for the project
- how much it will cost
- whether you can afford it now, or whether you need to wait and build it in as a major project in the coming year.

3　Communicate and consult

Think carefully about how to communicate with employees about the planned job evaluation project. Damage control at the start is preferable to damage limitation later. Explore what others will read into the introduction of job evaluation, and consult wherever it is appropriate. If you need to talk to trade unions, start straight away; sell the benefits and try to work towards an agreement that is acceptable to all sides.

Communicate clearly, so that all employees understand what is happening, why, when and with what aim, and who is doing it. This will help to gain acceptance of the scheme.

4　Draw up a project plan

Remember that there are three basic elements to the process of job evaluation:

- scheme design
- data collection
- data analysis.

List and time all actions so you are clear about the order in which each step must be taken, what must precede each step, what depends on it and the main milestones along the way. Set a realistic timetable.

Draw up a separate plan for managing change issues, as the scheme may constitute a fairly significant change. Consider its implications in terms of change management. What sort of resistance are you likely to encounter? Which factors will help you and which will hinder you? Who can act as change agents or champions to help spread the word?

5 Implement the scheme

If you are using an experienced external consultant, they will be able to advise you on what has to be done and how to go about it. If you are paying for their expertise, make sure you use it.

If you are handling the scheme in-house, follow your project and change management plans.

If it has been agreed that employee representatives are to participate in the introduction of job evaluation, this can be done effectively through a job evaluation committee. The committee is normally made up of equal numbers of representatives from employees and management, but it should operate as a team and not as a negotiating body.

An appeals procedure should be set up for employees who dispute their grading and there should be a mechanism for evaluating new jobs or changes in jobs.

6 Monitor the scheme

After the lengthy process of design and implementation, be wary of the scheme taking on a life of its own and becoming rigid. Just as jobs will continue to evolve or change, so their content will have an impact on the scheme framework you have devised.

Monitor and maintain the scheme as jobs change and new ones are created. You may need a panel or team, trained in job evaluation techniques, to meet regularly to carry out re-evaluations.

As a manager you should avoid:

● imagining that job evaluation will automatically save money – it is a process designed to sort out relativities and positions within an overall structure rather than to limit pay

- forgetting that even the most analytical system needs judgement and a human touch to refine scientific results and make them workable

- thinking that job evaluation is an exact science and the assessment of job demands can ever be totally objective

- believing that job evaluation determines actual pay and that it eliminates the need for negotiations in pay and conditions or differentials between grades

- allowing any bias on grounds of race, sex, disability, sexual orientation, religion/belief or age to creep into the evaluation.

Performance management

Michael Armstrong and Angela Baron, two well-known writers on human resource management, define performance management as 'a process which contributes to the effective management of individuals and teams in order to achieve high levels of organisational performance. As such, it establishes shared understanding about what is to be achieved and an approach to leading and developing people which will ensure that it is achieved.' They stress that it is 'a strategy which relates to every activity of the organisation set in the context of its human resource policies, culture, style and communications systems'.

Performance management is an integrated approach to helping an organisation achieve its aims and objectives by monitoring and improving the performance of individuals, departments and the organisation as a whole. This checklist aims to provide an understanding of the principles of performance management. It outlines the main issues to be considered in the introduction and operation of a performance management scheme at organisational level, and provides guidance for individuals on how to take advantage of performance management to improve their personal performance and develop their potential. A performance management system uses agreed targets and objectives to enable managers to measure and review performance, giving a clear indication as to whether the activities undertaken by individuals are contributing to the achievement of organisational goals.

Current levels of performance are not always what an organisation and its employees would like them to be. Individuals can work to narrow this gap by becoming more productive, developing their skills, or becoming better informed; organisations can improve processes, systems and procedures. To be effective, performance review must be conducted in the context of an organisation's overall strategic plan, with the aim of generating the momentum required to achieve corporate goals.

Effective performance management should always include pre-planned elements supported by informal reviews as appropriate. At times, it may be helpful to bring in external assistance, or to consider 360 degree feedback for individuals and groups. Performance management should always be a shared process between employees and managers.

Performance management involves:

- understanding current practice
- identifying future or intended practice
- recognising the processes and driving forces which will improve performance
- agreeing targets and objectives to meet organisational goals
- using tools, techniques, support from managers and colleagues, and training and development activities to develop capabilities and achieve the desired progress
- measuring and monitoring changes, improvements and progress towards goals
- reviewing progress, renewing goals and moving on.

Action checklist: organisational level

1 Align objectives with organisational strategy

The purpose, values and goals of each unit or department of the organisation should support or relate to the purpose, values and goals of the organisation. This will create a situation where each time a departmental goal is achieved, the organisation moves forward.

2 Set standards, criteria, indicators

Competitiveness requires organisations to stay in touch or benchmark with best practice, or best in class. Benchmarking will enable you to compare your key processes with similar processes in other industries. For example, if prompt telephone answering is a key process, look to organisations in service industries such as the AA, or another high-profile organisation that excels in that process.

All standards and indicators should be SMART (specific, measurable, achievable, realistic, timely or time-bound).

As individual performance management grades are often linked to salary levels, organisations need be clear about the standards that will apply to each grade. It can be demotivating and counter-productive, for example, if an unqualified achievement of agreed objectives does not lead to the award of the highest grade, because the company has predetermined the percentage of people who will be awarded the highest grade in any particular year. Honest management of expectations is fundamentally important for the credibility of the process.

3 Choose evaluation methods

Output-based evaluation is more useful than a ranking or rating system with criteria that are vague, or subjective. Performance management is about helping people to improve, but there may come a time when, after all possible support and encouragement have been given, performance is simply unsatisfactory. In this case remedial or even disciplinary action may be necessary. When selecting evaluation methods, keep the purpose for which they are to be used clearly in mind. This is particularly important when performance management is used to inform decisions on pay.

4 Assess the suitability of quality/customer care programmes

When implementing performance management, take account of the quality management programmes currently in place and review their suitability. For example, ISO 9000 quality systems are perhaps best suited to stable operations that are not undergoing radical change. *Kaizen*, as a continuous improvement scheme, is a more philosophical approach to improvement than a prescriptive system. The Business Excellence Model provides an adaptable framework for setting realistic and challenging standards.

5 Build performance appraisals into the business planning cycle

As performance management is dealing with personal objectives that feed into the organisation's strategy for achieving its corporate objectives, performance appraisals should become an integral part of the business planning cycle, particularly in relation to the delivery of products and services.

6 Ensure clear communication

Successful performance management depends on the engagement and involvement of all employees, so good communication about all aspects of the scheme – what it is seeking to achieve, how it will operate, how objectives will be set, what criteria will be used for evaluating performance and whether there is a link to pay or bonuses – is essential. A culture of open communication across the whole organisation is crucial. This will provide feedback to enable management to detect and prioritise, realistically, where and when performance criteria need to be adjusted.

7 Monitor and review

Continue to monitor and review the operation of the performance management scheme. All organisations operate within dynamic environments and changing circumstances may make adjustments necessary. Take note, also, of any problems that arise and make amendments to improve the operation of the scheme.

Action checklist: individual level

1 Identify where you are

An objective assessment of how you are currently performing forms the starting point. This means that you must have a clear idea of what you are expected to deliver, to what standard, and by when. A personal SWOT analysis (strengths, weaknesses, opportunities, threats) can help here, but a regular communication process with line managers is the best approach. Colleagues and peers can also help in assessing your performance. Make a clear record of your current position so that later on you can assess what improvements have been made.

2 Identify where you want/need to be

This may be to perform a task better or faster, or to carry out a new task. It may mean learning new skills or acquiring knowledge, capitalising on present strengths or tackling an individual weakness. This position needs to be describable and preferably measurable. Be mindful that there may be some degree of divergence between what you as the individual 'want' to do and what the organisation 'needs' you to do – for example, in terms of skills for the current job role versus skills for your career in the longer term.

3 Agree objectives and indicators

Objectives should be agreed between you and your line manager in line with organisational and departmental goals, and the criteria by which performance will be judged should be agreed, not imposed. Make sure that you will be able to measure progress towards the agreed objectives and that the indicators set will give you a direct insight into whether you are improving your efficiency or effectiveness. For example, if a plan to deliver outputs is agreed with your line manager, an indicator for efficiency would be the extent to which you stick to the plan; an indicator of effectiveness would be the level of success in delivering the outputs. Setting standards or indicators for some tasks can be straightforward and based on time, accuracy and productivity. Other 'softer' areas such as personal skills development are not so easy to quantify.

4 Make use of relevant tools and techniques

A number of tools can be used to monitor progress, identify shortcomings, and even measure how well you are performing. Fishbone (Ishikawa) diagrams and input–output diagrams are useful for qualitative progress; Pareto analysis, moving averages and the CUSUM (cumulative sum control chart) technique are more suited to quantitative measures. But don't forget that an honest and open discussion between you and your line manager remains an effective way to assess your progress. Record the main elements of the conversation on an official appraisal/review form, and jointly agree and sign it off.

5 Test and trial

Having worked out the causes of shortcomings in your performance, consider whether to opt for the simplest, cheapest, most efficient, most easily understood solution, the one that will elicit the most support, or the solution likely to have the greatest impact. The latter is not necessarily the best; take things one step at a time and reflect and adapt as you go.

6 Evaluate performance

The evaluation of performance is a key stage, making all the effort worthwhile. What and how you evaluate depend on the standards and objectives agreed. Meeting a budget or sales target will be easy to identify. Hitting a target objective – or progress towards it – is also measurable. In softer skills acquisition, sometimes gut feeling will tell you how near or far you are from the target. Performance evaluation should be carried out on a regular basis, and both line manager and report must be aware of or agree on the timeframe at the beginning of each reporting year. Mid-year reviews will also be helpful to improve the quality of work throughout the year and to make any necessary adjustments.

7 Carry out performance appraisals

Performance appraisals should include the points covered in 1–6 above. Learning and development needs should also be addressed. A personal development plan can be helpful in identifying development needs, making plans to meet these, recording development activities and demonstrating what has been learnt.

As a manager you should avoid:

- taking an 'all-or-nothing' approach – build incrementally on knowledge and experience
- being rigid or adopting a 'command-and-control' approach to goal setting
- looking for a quick fix
- giving employees 'surprises' related to poor performance – problems need to be addressed at an early stage
- neglecting 'soft' issues such as building relationships and giving feedback.

Using 360 degree feedback

360 degree feedback (or appraisal) involves appraisal by those above, below and at the same level as the appraisee and incorporates self-assessment. In practice, it may not include all these elements. Depending on the level of openness required, feedback may be provided through a third party, so that the opinions of particular individuals cannot be identified. Similar approaches are described in a glossary towards the end of this checklist.

360 degree feedback is most often used in development or for measuring the impact of training and to a lesser extent in performance appraisal. It has particular relevance for appraising leadership skills.

Changes in organisational structures towards flatter hierarchies and greater employee empowerment have had implications for the appraisal process. Individual managers often have a greater span of control, so an employee's colleagues may be in a better position to judge his or her performance than before. Hence the now established interest in 360 degree feedback, which, by combining the perspectives of subordinates, peers and team members can provide a well-rounded and more accurate and objective view than the perceptions of a single person. 360 degree feedback can be particularly motivating for people who undervalue themselves. It can also increase general awareness of the impact people have on each other and lead to more open working relationships and improved teamwork. It is most effective in organisations that have, or are moving towards, an open, supportive and participative culture.

While making the assumption that schemes will be managed by HR professionals rather than individual line managers, this checklist provides an introduction, designed to give readers a clear understanding of the management and operation of 360 degree feedback and the principles involved.

Action checklist

1 Decide which behaviours you want to measure and whom to assess

Consider which sets of knowledge, skills and abilities you want to measure – for example, should they be competency-based, job-related, or behaviour-related? Remember that 360 degree feedback can be used at any level of the organisation, so decide whether you want to assess specific individuals, particular teams, particular levels, or the whole organisation.

2 Design a feedback questionnaire

Devise the detailed questions or, if you do not have the necessary expertise in-house, consider the options of buying in a ready-made questionnaire or employing a consultant. The use of an online questionnaire is worth considering, as this can reduce administration, increase the quality of feedback, and improve accuracy and confidentiality. Check that the questions are phrased to elicit a descriptive, rather than a judgemental, response, as the former is less likely to give offence and more likely to provide information for the appraisee to act upon. Also avoid asking questions which the majority of the likely appraisers are not qualified to answer or which contain terms that might be open to misinterpretation.

3 Communicate the scheme and prepare participants

Good communication and an open management style are crucial to the success of 360 degree feedback. Make sure that the scope and purpose of the scheme are clearly explained and encourage employees to express any concerns they have. If necessary, circulate a pilot questionnaire asking employees for their views on managers in the organisation in general, for example. This will demonstrate how the scheme will work and give reassurance. A focus on strengths as much as weaknesses will help to make the exercise non-threatening. Appoint a manager to act as a facilitator and publicise the person's roles and responsibilities. This should be someone who is widely respected and has a reputation for fairness and honesty. If it is not appropriate to nominate an internal manager, consider using a consultant.

4 Train all appraisers in giving, and appraisees in receiving, feedback

Encourage appraisers to be constructive, positive and specific, rather than critical, negative and vague. In describing a colleague's behaviour, for example, 'I notice that you rarely acknowledge us when you arrive in the morning' is more helpful than 'I think you are a bad communicator'. 'I note that you need time and space to yourself, but when you get it you can really produce the goods' pinpoints the message in an acceptable way, which should be better received than 'You're too much of a loner'. Do not allow the appraisal to become an opportunity for subjective gripes. When this happens, those who receive a critical appraisal will often get their own back when appraising others, especially if they are identified or identifiable.

5 Let appraisees choose their appraisers

Allow employees to choose who is to appraise them from an agreed pool, but encourage them to select people who know them and the work they do, not just those with whom they get on well. The aim is to achieve a rounded appraisal. Set limits on the number involved in each appraisal – otherwise the exercise can become administratively difficult. Instruct appraisers to return their questionnaires to the appointed facilitator. If it has been agreed that all comments will be treated anonymously, reassure them that their views will not be attributed to them. Minimise the time period between collecting the data and giving the results.

6 Decide how feedback is to be presented

Work out how the results are to be collated and presented by the facilitator. Is your objective to allow employees to compare their own performance over time, compare themselves with like employees, or compare themselves against a set of competences? Consider whether feedback on particular actions is to be linked to the importance of the action to the job. If so, the results will need to be weighted accordingly.

7 Provide counselling and assistance

Decide whether measures for improvement should be left to individuals or whether they should be offered solutions. If you wish individuals to take responsibility for their own improvement, don't show the results to their boss without their approval. The facilitator or another trained person such as a psychologist should be available to help employees deal with feedback, particularly to advise on how to deal with diverging views. Consider whether to hold development sessions in which appraisees can offer support to each other.

8 Set action plans for improvement

Follow up appraisal with a programme of suitable training. This may range from attending a course or sitting with a colleague, to internal or external secondment. Remember that learners will have different needs and preferences.

9 Evaluate the use of 360 degree feedback

Evaluate the appraisal initiative, taking into account the thoughts of all participants, including any difficulties that arose in completing the appraisal questionnaire or in analysing the data from it. Compare the results of using 360 degree feedback with previous appraisal schemes. Details from the evaluation should be acknowledged when undertaking the next appraisal.

Glossary

Peer appraisal: employees are evaluated by their colleagues and their supervisor.

Team appraisal: team members assess the performance of members of their own team. Feedback should preferably also come from representatives of team clients and from a supervisor.

Upward feedback: managers are appraised by those who report to them.

As a manager you should avoid:

- forgetting that employees may find the introduction of 360 degree feedback both threatening and challenging
- treating 360 degree feedback as a one-off exercise or leaving long gaps between appraisals
- allowing appraisers to drift into personal attacks
- generating an environment of suspicion.

Rosabeth Moss Kanter
Pioneer of empowerment and change management

Introduction

It is difficult to classify Rosabeth Moss Kanter as a specialist in any particular area, as her prolific writings encompass a wide range of topics. She views herself, however, as a thought leader and developer of ideas, and is best known for her work on change management and innovation.

Much of Kanter's success is due to a combination of rigorous research, practical experience and her ability to write in a clear and concrete way, using many illustrative examples.

Life and career

Kanter was born in 1943, in Cleveland, Ohio, and attended the top women's academy, Bryn Mawr. She took her PhD at the University of Michigan and was associate professor of sociology at Brandeis University from 1966 to 1977. Between 1973 and 1974 Kanter was on the Organizational Behavior programme at Harvard, and she was a fellow and visiting scholar of Harvard Law School between 1975 and 1976.

From 1977 to 1986, Kanter was professor of sociology and professor of organisational management at Yale, and from 1979 to 1986 she was a visiting professor at the Sloan School of Management, Massachusetts Institute of Technology (MIT). In 1986, she returned to Harvard as the 'class of 1960' professor of entrepreneurship and innovation, and she currently holds the Ernest L. Arbuckle professorship at Harvard Business School, where she specialises in strategy, innovation and leadership for change.

Between 1989 and 1992, Kanter was editor of *Harvard Business Review*, and she acted as an economic adviser to Michael Dukakis during his 1988 presidential campaign. She has travelled widely as a public speaker, lecturer and international consultant. In 1977, she and future husband Barry Stein set up a management consultancy, Goodmeasure Inc, which has some large and well-known multinational companies as clients.

Key texts

Kanter has authored or co-authored several books and well over 150 major articles. Her doctoral thesis was on communes and her first books, written during the early 1970s, were sociological. The three books for which she is best known are *Men and Women of the Corporation*, *The Change Masters* and *When Giants Learn to Dance*. There is a logical progression within them, in that the first studies the stifling effects of bureaucratic organisation on individuals, while the subsequent titles go on to explore ways in which flatter, 'post-entrepreneurial' organisations release, and make use of, individuals' talents and abilities. All three were extremely successful.

Later books include *The Challenge of Organizational Change* (with Barry A. Stein and Todd D. Jick), *World Class: Thriving Locally in the Global Economy* and *The Frontiers of Management and Confidence*.

Men and Women of the Corporation

Men and Women of the Corporation won the C. Wright Mills Award in 1977 as the year's best book on social issues. It is a detailed analysis of the nature and effects of the distribution of power and powerlessness within the headquarters of one large, bureaucratic, multinational corporation (called Industrial Supply Corporation, or Indsco, in the book). The effects of powerlessness on behaviour are explored and the detrimental effects of disempowerment, for both the organisation and individual employees, are made clear. Women were the most obvious group affected by lack of power, though Kanter emphasises that other groups outside the white, male norm, such as individuals from the ethnic minorities, were also affected.

Three main structural variables explained the behaviours observed within Indsco:

● the structure of opportunity

● the structure of power

● the proportional distribution of people of different kinds.

Before this book was published, it was generally assumed that behavioural differences underlay women's general lack of career progress. Kanter's findings made structural issues central, however, and the implications for change management were significant. If all employees were to become more empowered, according to Kanter's analysis, organisations rather than people would need to change. Accordingly, the book ends with practical policy suggestions to create appropriate structural changes.

While working on this book, Kanter identified the need for organisational change to improve working life, create more equal opportunities and make more use of employees' talents within organisations.

The Change Masters

In *The Change Masters*, approaches to achieving these ends were put forward. Kanter compares four traditional corporations like Indsco with six competitive and successful organisations, described as change masters. All findings were weighed against the experiences of many other companies, and much other material. From the six innovative organisations, Kanter derives a model for encouraging innovation.

Innovative companies were found to have a distinct, 'integrative' approach to management, while firms unlikely to innovate were described as 'segmentalist' in being compartmentalised by units or departments. The difference begins with a company's approach to problem solving, and extends through its structure and culture. Entrepreneurial organisations:

- operate at the edge of their competence, focusing on exploring the unknown rather than on controlling the known

- measure themselves by future-focused visions (how far they have to go) rather than by past standards (how far they have come).

Three clusters of structures and processes are identified as factors that encourage power circulation and access to power: open communication systems, network-forming arrangements and decentralisation of resources. Their practical implementation is discussed.

Individuals can also be change masters. 'New entrepreneurs' are people who improve existing businesses rather than start new ones. They can be found in any functional area and are described as, literally, the right people, in the right place, at the right time:

- right people – vision and ideas extending beyond the organisation's normal practice

- right place – an integrative environment fostering proactive vision, coalitions and teams

- right time – moments in the historic flow when change becomes most possible.

The ultimate change masters are corporate leaders, who translate their vision into a new organisational reality.

The Change Masters advocates 'participation management' as the means to greater empowerment. Some major building blocks for productive change are identified, and practical measures to remove road blocks to innovation are discussed.

When Giants Learn to Dance

When Giants Learn to Dance completes Kanter's trilogy on the need for change which, she considered, US corporations had to confront and manage in order to compete more effectively. The book is based on observation from within various organisations, through consultancy projects. The global economy is likened to a 'corporate Olympics' of competing businesses, with results determining which nations, as well as which organisations, are winners.

The games differ, but successful teams share some characteristics such as strength, skill, discipline, good organisation and focus on individual excellence. To win, American companies are having to become progressively more entrepreneurial and less bureaucratic. The 'post-entrepreneurial' corporation is put forward as a model for the 1990s, fostered by the three shaping forces of:

- context set at the top
- top management values
- project ideas and approaches coming up through the organisation.

Such an 'athletic' organisation is lean, flexible and able to do more with less, and it seeks to create synergies through the use of team and partnership approaches. The organisation is built on empowerment, and employees are highly valued within team-based or partnership relationships.

Seven skills or sensibilities of individual 'business athletes' are given as:

- ability to operate and get results without depending on hierarchical authority, position or status
- ability to compete in a way that enhances cooperation and aims to achieve high standards rather than destroy competitors
- high ethical standards to support the trust which is crucial for cooperative approaches when competing in the corporate Olympics

- a dose of humility, with basic self-confidence tempered by the understanding that new things will always need to be learnt
- process focus, with respect to the process of implementation as well as the substance of what is implemented
- multifaceted and ambidextrous approach to support cross-functional or cross-departmental work, alliances where appropriate, and the cutting of ties where necessary
- satisfaction in results, and willingness to be rewarded according to achievements.

World Class: Thriving Locally in the Global Economy

This book focuses on world-class companies with employees described as 'cosmopolitan' in type. These people are wealthy in terms of the 'three Cs' – concepts, competence and connections – and carry a more universal culture to all the places in which their company operates.

This knowledge-rich breed is set against 'locals' who are set in their ways, and the two groups are viewed as the main classes in modern society. The book is optimistic, in that Kanter believes stakeholders can influence world-class companies to spread best practices around the world.

Globalisation, it is argued, offers an opportunity to develop businesses and give new life to the regions. From her studies of regenerative areas, Kanter suggests that business and local government leaders can work together to draw in the right sort of companies to create prosperity.

European as well as American successes are used to illustrate the benefits of globalisation and the centrality of regional economies.

The Challenge of Organizational Change: How Companies Experience it and Leaders Guide it

Co-authored with Barry A. Stein and Todd D. Jick, this is a book on the management of change, which is filled with practical examples. In line with many other writings on managing change, a distinction is drawn between evolutionary and revolutionary change, here described as 'long march' and 'bold stroke' approaches.

Rosabeth Moss Kanter on the Frontiers of Management

This collects Kanter's essays and research articles for *Harvard Business Review* into one volume.

Confidence: How Winning Streaks and Losing Streaks Begin and End

In this book Kanter explores the culture and dynamics of high-performance organisations compared with those in decline by explaining how confidence produces success in all types of situations. Drawing upon the experiences of sports teams, the perspective of the cycle of confidence is developed. This helps to explain why confidence grows in winning teams and propels a tradition of success, while confidence erodes in losing streaks and its absence makes it hard to stop losing. This thinking is applied to the business environment, and Kanter shows how confidence is the key to thinking big and bold rather than small and tentative.

A framework for turning confidence around is presented:

● The first stone – facing facts and reinforcing responsibility

● The second stone – cultivating collaboration

● The third stone – inspiring initiative and innovation.

Numerous sports and business examples are used to illustrate these ideas, and Kanter concludes by exploring the role of leaders in building confidence and the personal life lessons for individuals.

In perspective

Kanter has the ability to present some fairly complex ideas in a way that many people seem to find accessible. Her books are well-argued, well-illustrated and supported with a wealth of practical research evidence. But above all they are readable and engaging. Some of her central ideas, once viewed by some as unrealistic, have now become absorbed into general management wisdom. These include empowerment, participative management and employee involvement. Despite being over three decades old, her earlier works retain a freshness and relevance for today's business environment.

In *The Frontiers of Management*, she is presented as a groundbreaking explorer who has initiated a revolution in terms of new ways of working. It is also pointed out, however, that some managers have still not crossed the frontiers, or do so in aspiration rather than actuality.

Talent management

In its broadest terms talent management is defined as the selection, development, engagement and retention of individuals who are seen to be of particular value to an organisation.

There are differing perspectives on what constitutes talent, some focusing on gifted high-fliers and others on the collective capacity of employees within an organisation. In both cases the term refers to people who have the potential to make a significant impact.

A talent management system is an official policy clearly defining the criteria and processes for identifying, developing and retaining talented employees.

The development of talented employees can be one of the most profitable investments an organisation makes. As long-term organisational performance is achieved primarily through a focus on people, it is fundamental that talented personnel are identified, nurtured and, most importantly, retained within an organisation. Investment in 'human capital' develops the skills, knowledge and vision needed to take an organisation forward and can help to meet strategic objectives, maintain competitive advantage within the marketplace, and ensure the long-term success and viability of the organisation. The development of a pool of talent offers an organisation the flexibility to select the best managers for current market conditions and for the future, allowing for fluctuations in business growth and changes in market conditions.

Talent management is primarily geared to creating a people and organisational management capability within middle and senior management. It is considered to be a priority for senior management. Talent management encompasses not just the recruitment process but also performance management, management development, succession planning and organisation capability.

A tailored talent management system benefits the whole organisation in engaging employees, supporting high performance, enhancing corporate image and helping the organisation to become an employer of choice, as well as contributing to diversity management and reducing recruitment costs.

There is no one way to approach talent management. Organisations of different sizes and types, in different sectors, and with differing aims and objectives will have different needs and aspirations, which their talent management systems should address. Each organisation needs to adopt a strategic approach that suits its particular requirements. In some organisations talent management processes cover the whole workforce; in others a more segmented and exclusive approach is taken; and in others a combination of the two approaches is used. This checklist outlines common principles, which should be followed in any talent management system.

Action checklist

1 Develop a talent management system

A talent management system needs to be put in place and embedded into a long-term business plan for the organisation to successfully select, develop and retain talented employees. As well as ensuring the identification of potential candidates for development, a well-planned system demonstrates an organisation's commitment to talent management and keeps 'talent' high on the corporate agenda. Identify relevant strategic perspectives to suit organisation requirements – for example, process, cultural, competitive, developmental, HR planning or change management perspectives. To identify leaders who will lead the business into its next phase of development, a consideration of the immediate, as well as the long-term needs of the organisation is essential. Don't forget that individuals develop at differing rates and at different stages, and keep late developers in mind.

A holistic approach to talent management should be taken by seeking out individuals who will benefit the whole organisation. Make sure that expectations are clearly communicated to employees and that the policy is seen to be fair and reasonable. Don't raise any expectations you will be unable to meet.

2 Work collaboratively

When formulating a cohesive talent management system, collaborate with all the parties whose involvement is crucial.

- Talent management needs to be supported from the top; the involvement of **senior management** and the **chief executive officer** (CEO) demonstrates the organisation's commitment to managing talent.

- **Human resources managers** are at the forefront of attracting and recruiting talented employees.

- **Line managers** are responsible for the development and retention of talented personnel.

Working in conjunction with others ensures that the talent management system will be implemented effectively to facilitate the internal growth of the organisation.

3 Recruit and select the right candidates for the right jobs

Identify talent for today and for the future, and select individuals who show the potential to grow. Look for individuals who have a people focus, will listen, are open-minded, can nurture, can be decisive and are able to communicate an organisation's vision. Select people who will learn quickly and grow as leaders. Candidates should respect and adhere to the organisation's values. Monitor the performance of possible candidates in their current role to provide an indication of how they will perform in the future. Be aware of whether individuals are willing to be mobile, moving either within the organisation or to another geographical location.

4 Become an attractive employer

Becoming a desirable employer will help to attract good people. This is not just a matter of offering higher salaries and more extensive benefit packages than other employers, although it is important to be seen to be paying a fair rate for the job. Factors such as an attractive working environment, regard for work–life balance, a culture of cooperation and respect, and opportunities for development and promotion are also crucial. This will assist not only in attracting talent, but retaining it as well.

5 Develop talented personnel

The development of star performers should be fostered and nurtured. Engage with employees by keeping them stimulated, challenged and motivated. There are various mechanisms organisations can employ to ensure that talented staff are successfully developed and stimulated.

- Support development by providing coaching and/or mentoring. Consider the selection and use of an effective mentor for every talented performer, ideally someone from outside their line-management structure and with the skills, experience and reputation that would make them a credible source of guidance, support and challenge.

- Identify training and development needs that will provide the necessary criteria for continuing professional development.

- Offer professional qualifications which provide formal accreditation for an employee's progress and achievements.

- Consider fast-track programmes by instigating accelerated routes to promotion as a method of recognition and stimulation.

- Management training schemes, project work, secondments, shadowing and transfers are a means of developing and broadening knowledge and enhancing variety and stimulation.
- Create attractive goals to aim for, such as admittance into an organisation's talent pool.
- Facilitate networking opportunities.

6 Retain talented personnel

If a talented employee is an asset to your company, he or she will be valuable to competitors too. Therefore, once recruitment has been successfully achieved, it is essential that the talent remains in your organisation. So how do you dissuade talented individuals from seeking new challenges with a competitor? Everyone wants to feel that their contribution is recognised and valued by the organisation. Making people feel appreciated will enhance motivation and commitment.

The attitudes and behaviour of direct line managers play a fundamental role here and can provide a key to retaining and developing star performers.

- Develop talent by providing the support and guidance needed to help each individual reach their full potential.
- Provide frequent, constructive and honest feedback on performance to accelerate development.
- Line managers should establish an employee's career drivers. This will provide a developmental framework by which to work.
- Individuals should play a part in negotiating their own development needs and career paths.
- Set targets, in both the short and long term, so that a clear development route is evident to both the employer and the employee.
- Identify areas for development and/or improvement to foster talent, ensuring that any 'gaps' are adequately addressed.

Ensuring equality of opportunity and transparency over criteria for

entry into talent and development programmes will complement
diversity initiatives as well as support retention.

7 Devise measurement strategies

Considerable effort, time and money have been invested in the
selection, development and retention of talented staff. So, as
with any company outlay, it is important that the investment is
appropriately monitored and recorded. To assess the return
on investment (ROI), measurement strategies need to be put
in place. The evaluation methods should form part of the wider
talent management system. Design suitable and economical
metrical systems to effectively calculate your investment.
Monitoring and measuring the performance of personnel through
professional development reviews and associated appraisal
schemes can assist with identifying gaps and recognising the
additional training and support required.

8 Utilise the talent management system

The recruitment of individuals with the skills and vision to take an
organisation forward can act as a catalyst. Individuals who have
the skills and knowledge to act as change agents can initiate
change by sharing their ideas with the existing workforce.

As a manager you should avoid:

- devising talent management systems without the involvement of
  crucial players within the organisation
- alienating the rest of the workforce if it is perceived that certain
  members are being given preferential treatment
- selecting personnel who are outstanding in their own role but who
  cannot work as part of a team
- overlooking personality traits of promising individuals which may
  cause problems at a later date
- waiting until an employee 'shines' rather than identifying their
  potential early on

- promoting a promising individual too soon just because a senior vacancy has arisen

- formulating a development and training plan without first consulting the employee

- focusing purely on the organisation's current status – consider its future objectives as well when identifying potential candidates for promotion.

Succession planning

Succession planning is preparation for the replacement of key post holders, in advance of resignation or retirement. It involves identifying the new post holder and preparing them for the role through development activities. Succession planning is more specific in its focus than talent management and tends to concentrate on key positions within senior management, including the chief executive officer and board members. Succession planning processes are also used for other roles within an organisation. These may include relatively junior posts, especially in small and medium-sized businesses.

Traditionally, succession planning was carried out in a relatively stable environment. Internal candidates were reviewed by the HR director or the chief executive, who then made recommendations to the board which were invariably accepted. The evolution of a more dynamic business environment, with increasing skill shortages and flatter organisational structures, has led to a need for more flexible succession planning processes. In the UK, a growing trend for working beyond the normal retirement age and the phasing out of the default retirement age during 2011 have provided additional challenges for succession planning.

The relationship between succession planning and talent management has not always been clear, but succession planning is increasingly being linked with talent management strategies. In practice, a number of different approaches are used for succession planning. Organisations have different cultures and strategies and each will need to decide on the best way to manage succession when employees move on or retire. The most common model for succession planning involves planning for key senior posts only. A devolved model plans for key posts throughout an organisation. The elements of the succession planning process are similar for both approaches.

Action checklist

1 Align succession planning processes with wider talent management initiatives and business needs

To facilitate this, a close working relationship should be established between senior management and the HR department. Succession planning should be led and coordinated by the HR director with the involvement of the chief executive. The process involves:

- anticipating the loss of key personnel
- evaluating the effectiveness of current key personnel
- highlighting the strengths and weaknesses of the available talent pool
- developing talent in preparation for greater responsibility
- keeping succession plans up-to-date
- generating background data
- monitoring performance trends and the expectations of individuals.

2 Consider the scope of the succession planning process

This relates to:

- the posts for which successors need to be identified
- the groups of individuals to be considered
- the job routes which individuals need to follow in preparation for appointment to a senior role

- the managers who will contribute to the planning process.

3 Produce person and post plans

Person plans look at the range of jobs that might be suitable for a particular person. Both short-term jobs and longer-term potential should be indicated, together with specific development plans and requirements.

Typically, a post plan records:

- type of job
- level
- function
- role
- geographic and organisational location
- key characteristics required, including any that are mandatory or highly desirable, for example professional qualifications or language skills
- position status – date of changeover
- short-term successors
- long-term successors.

Create and maintain a database to hold this information and use a consistent approach to coding job features. This will help in effective candidate searching and the identification of any obvious training needs in the leading candidates.

4 The move from jobs to roles

Increasingly, succession planning involves developing and identifying job groups from which successors can be chosen for a number of roles. In this way the skills required for a particular job group can be developed and a talent pool established.

5 Integrate succession plans with existing competency frameworks

The use of management competency frameworks in assessing skills required for a senior role can be helpful, but additional methods of assessing leadership skills such as diagnostic tests and assessment centres may also be used.

6 Ask heads of functions or divisions to contribute to succession planning

This can be done by:

- identifying short-term successors for posts which have been unexpectedly vacated

- considering potential successors within their own areas who also might be long-term successors

- offering their thoughts on the quality of candidates available

- considering alternative candidates or runners-up for the post or posts

- commenting on the suitability of candidates for alternative posts

- communicating apparent skills gaps and proposing how they might be closed

- commenting on their ability to recruit externally

- looking at the effect of business changes on demand for talent.

However, be aware that some departmental leaders may be unwilling to release good people or even try to hide them because of the contribution they are making in their current role. Central oversight of succession planning must endeavour to ensure that such people are redeployed for the greater good of the organisation.

7 Consider the fit between a potential successor and the organisation's culture

Organisational culture, politics and strategy must be considered when appointing successors. A good fit between the individual and the organisational culture can help ensure a smooth transition and enable the organisation to move ahead without being deflected from its aims and objectives. In some cases, however, an outsider with a fresh approach may be needed to revitalise and redirect an organisation for future success. Succession planning is about more than capabilities, however impressive the individual's track record may be.

8 Move towards greater transparency and openness

More openness should be encouraged with better communication on where the process fits with other HR processes. Feedback opportunities should be available to those individuals discussed as part of the succession process.

9 Reach a shared view of talent and post requirements

Senior managers responsible for succession, usually the board of directors, should form a succession committee and conduct an overall review, including looking at the current cycle of plans and how they are progressing. This will enable them to amend and confirm development and succession plans. The committee should be especially concerned where there is no obvious field of candidates for a senior post due to fall vacant in two or three years' time. It may be necessary to accelerate the development of one or more potential candidates to avoid an interregnum that might damage the organisation.

The succession planning process should be well disciplined and systematic, but it must incorporate a degree of flexibility. With the abolition of a default retirement age, it can no longer be assumed that all individuals will retire at the same age. Personal circumstances may also change unexpectedly, leading to situations such as the loss of key post holders which will need to be addressed at short notice.

10 **Managing and planning CEO succession**

Traditionally, it is the role of the chair to consider and manage the process of succession for CEOs. Finding a successor to the CEO is the responsibility of the board of directors. The role the current CEO plays in managing their own succession will depend on the strategic direction the organisation wishes to take. There can be risks in allowing the CEO to take control and choose a successor in their own image.

As a manager you should avoid:

- letting the CEO take too much control of their own succession
- ignoring the relationship between succession planning and talent management
- allowing personal interests and egos to infiltrate the succession planning process
- allowing the succession planning process to become too mechanistic.

Training needs analysis

A training need is an individual, team or organisational level requirement for skills or abilities which can be fulfilled through training, learning or development interventions.

A lack of adequate training can prevent employees from fulfilling their job responsibilities and hinder organisations in achieving their objectives. Training needs analysis (TNA) should aim to detect where and how this may be happening, and establish the need for training and development in specific areas.

The aim of TNA is to ensure that training addresses existing problems, is tailored to organisational objectives, and is delivered in an effective and cost-efficient manner.

TNA involves:

- monitoring current performance using techniques such as observation, interviews, regular performance appraisals and questionnaires
- anticipating future shortfalls or problems
- identifying the type and level of development required and analysing how this can best be provided.

Training needs fall into three broad types:

- those that can be anticipated
- those that are identified through monitoring and performance appraisals
- those that result from unexpected problems.

Providing effective learning, development and training opportunities depends on knowing what is required – for the individual, the team and the organisation as a whole. A training needs analysis to establish where training is needed is particularly important in the context of today's fast-changing environment: it will help to keep people's skills and abilities current and give organisations a competitive edge.

Analysing training needs is a vital first step for any effective training, enabling organisations to channel learning and development to where it is most needed to improve organisational performance. TNA is a natural function of appraisal systems and performance management, and is a key requirement for Investors in People, the UK's leading people management standard. It is also often required in the context of applications for funding or to meet service-level agreements.

Managers today are often at least partially responsible for developing their team, and it will help if they understand the principles of TNA, which requires systematic planning, analysis and coordination to ensure that organisational priorities are taken into account, duplication of effort is avoided and economies of scale are achieved. All potential trainees should be included in the TNA process and, ideally, managers should receive training on the process, and how they should approach and implement it.

This checklist outlines an approach for introducing TNA into an organisation. While most large organisations have already developed cultures of continuous improvement and self-managed continuing professional development for their employees, organisation-wide TNA can also be helpful in some circumstances, such as when new technology is being introduced on a wide scale.

Action checklist

1 Ensure that the identification of training needs is integrated across the organisation

Development needs discovered in one department are likely to exist in others. It is pointless for individual managers to throw their own limited resources at each problem as it arises, duplicating efforts and dissipating energy. Most organisations have an HR management function which organises overall training delivery. While managers may not be responsible for coordinating the system, they have an important role to play in collecting information on the training needs of their people, and passing it on to the HR or training department.

At the very least, managers can liaise with other colleagues to aggregate training needs information, so that a range of appropriate cross-departmental training and development activities can be planned.

2 Anticipate future needs

Development needs often emerge at organisational or activity level. For example, the introduction of a new software system may well have training implications for those who must work with it; or a strategic decision to enhance the level of customer service is likely to depend on a general programme of customer service-related training for its success.

Other factors to look out for are:

- overdependence on one or two individuals who hold vital skills or knowledge
- changes in products or policies
- overall changes in internal work processes
- new legislative requirements.

3 Develop monitoring techniques

Some training needs can go unnoticed because they develop gradually within an organisation. Active monitoring systems are essential to spot these and provide regular information on performance gaps and training needs.

Variance analysis is one approach to monitoring. This sounds technical, but it is a simple tool for monitoring budgets. When a budget is agreed, expected monthly expenditure is detailed. Any major variance from the forecast – up or down – triggers an investigation into why it happened and what the implications will be. This translates neatly into the identification of training needs.

For TNA purposes, the budget numbers are replaced by performance standards and indicators that should be as specific as possible. For example, for a 'soft' issue like customer satisfaction, a standard could be set that stipulates that 90% of customers should feel they receive excellent service. Carrying out customer satisfaction surveys will allow the measurement of any deviation from this standard.

Asking questions at appraisal interviews can act as a form of survey, as the same issues will be addressed throughout the organisation. The identification of development needs is one of the purposes of appraisal and performance reviews.

In addition to including questions about development needs at appraisal interviews, a worthwhile approach to investigating one-off problems is to interview employees and customers. Regularly ask a random sample of people for their views on the same set of questions relating to general performance, for instance customer satisfaction levels.

4 Investigate unexpected problems with care

Monitoring will indicate where gaps and problems exist. However, it is possible to make the wrong assumptions when faced with a particular set of circumstances. For instance, unusually rapid staff turnover in a small section may lead to an assumption that unsocial hours worked there are the issue. Exit interviews,

however, may indicate that the turnover is a result of cramped
working conditions and poor ventilation – issues that training
cannot resolve, even though the monitoring process has helped
identify the problem.

By contrast, it could be that:

- the behaviour of the section head is the root cause
- errors at the recruitment stage have led to the employment of
  unsuitable people.

In both cases there is a development need: in the first case for the
section head, and in the second for those doing the recruiting.

5 Identify the level of need

It could be that a development need is limited to a single
individual or activity, but it is more likely to be relevant for
a number of people, a whole department or across the
organisation. For example, if employees are found to be habitually
treating customers as a nuisance, their attitude needs to change.
In this case, giving one or two people customer services training
would address the training need at the wrong level, because
organisational development is needed rather than individual
training sessions.

6 Consider what type of training will be most appropriate

Consider whether training needs can be met by using internal
expertise or whether external help will be necessary. Remember
that formal internal or external training courses are not the only
option; approaches such as coaching, mentoring or informal
peer-to-peer training should also be considered. Technological
developments have opened up a wide range of e-learning and
blended learning options, including self-managed online learning
programmes. Take into account the number of people to be
trained and the resources available.

7 Take appropriate action

If the training needs are within your span of control, at individual or maybe at activity level, you can take action to meet the needs you have identified. If the needs are broader, you will need to make recommendations and proposals to those responsible for planning and implementing learning and development interventions in your organisation. This may involve drawing up a report specifying the needs you have identified, your recommendations for meeting them and the expected benefits of the interventions.

While this may conclude the training needs analysis, this is not the end of the training and development process. You need to ensure that the development undertaken has been effective and worthwhile for the individual and your organisation.

As a manager you should avoid:

- making snap assumptions about performance problems
- organising training without first establishing a need
- taking a one-size-fits-all approach
- focusing on obvious training needs, when systematic monitoring may reveal more urgent needs.

Evaluating training and learning

Evaluation is the analytical process of assessing the value of something. In the case of training, this focuses on whether the time and money spent on training have achieved the required results.

It has become common practice to relate investment in all areas of a business to the achievement of strategic business objectives; this applies equally to investment in training and development. Managers are often asked to demonstrate that an expected benefit or value for money has been achieved, and evaluating the effectiveness of training will help them do this.

It used to be considered adequate for participants at training events to complete an evaluation form or 'happy sheet' on which they recorded their views about the course and the trainer or facilitator. This approach is still widely used, but its benefits are severely limited as it fails to indicate whether anything useful was learned or how that knowledge will be put into practice in the workplace.

The most widely accepted model of training evaluation is the four levels of training evaluation developed by Donald L. Kirkpatrick. This looks at:

- **Reaction** – how learners react to the training undertaken
- **Learning** – increase in knowledge and intellectual capacity
- **Behaviour** – the impact on learners' behaviour and performance in the workplace

- **Results** – effects on business performance.

  More recent approaches have focused on measuring the return on investment of training and development, and evaluating the effectiveness of the training function and the culture of learning within an organisation.

  This checklist presents an approach to training evaluation which builds evaluation into a continuous cycle of:

- identifying training needs

- defining objectives

- delivering training to meet those needs and objectives

- assessing learners' reactions to the training

- seeking evidence of knowledge acquired and skills learned and of their implementation in the workplace

- measuring the effects of training on bottom-line results.

  In-depth evaluation can be difficult, but putting in place training objectives and indicators against which you can assess progress provides a key to assessing return on investment in training and development. The information gained from evaluation will feed back into the performance management process, support discussion of individuals' progress and development, and provide information about performance on which to base appropriate training plans and processes for the future.

  This checklist takes an organisational approach to training evaluation and provides key points to help managers build evaluation into their training/learning and development programmes and assess the effectiveness of training interventions. It is not intended to provide guidance for trainers on the assessment of their own programmes and performance.

Action checklist

1 Define what you want training to achieve

Start by thinking about what you want to achieve and identifying measurable objectives. Once training needs have been identified, quantify the results and outcomes you expect.

Where practical skills are concerned, it may be possible to specify and measure outcomes by occupational, organisational or national standards, or to define them yourself. For example:

- operate a machine safely
- use a graphics package
- set up a website
- construct widgets using a new technology
- explain the organisation's security policy to an auditor.

It is harder to set measurable targets, however, for events designed to contribute to continuing learning or behavioural change. Building up knowledge and experience in a specific area is fundamental to development but difficult to quantify. In these cases, work with the learner to specify expected outcomes – for example, a more effective selling behaviour.

2 Turn targets into objectives

Objectives tell you what is to be achieved, by when. They should be SMART (specific, measurable, achievable, realistic, timely or time-limited).

A training objective specifies what you can expect the learner to know or be able to do as a result of the training. This may be directly following the training, or at a set time after the training, allowing the learner time to incorporate the learning into their work.

If a skill is to be developed, the measure could be, for example, that within six weeks of the end of training, the learner will be able to type a ten-page report within an hour with no more than six mistakes.

When formulating objectives relating to gaining knowledge, avoid the word 'understand', because understanding is not measurable. Replace it with words like 'show', 'state', 'explain' or 'describe', which enable you to check that the learner has absorbed the knowledge to meet an objective.

3 **Make sure that everyone knows the objectives of training and development activities and is aware of how they will be measured**

'Everyone' includes:

● the learners, who should receive advance information in their joining instructions and via personal briefings from their manager

● their managers (if you are arranging the training on behalf of other departments), so they know what their team members should be able to do as a result of the training

● the trainers – this may sound obvious, but they need to design the training based on what it should achieve. If training is provided by an external organisation, check that the provider can meet the specified objectives.

4 **Design methods for comparing results with objectives**

The best way to do this is to get people together to come up with one agreed and consistent approach. It may involve a post-training action plan, a debriefing session on return to the workplace, forms, questionnaires, observation checklists, feedback meetings or statistical data. The crucial point is that you must design the assessment procedures at an early stage.

Immediate feedback is important, but performance improvements need to be assessed over a realistic time span – often weeks and sometimes months. This allows time for the training to be applied and practised, leading to the actual outcomes you want to evaluate.

5 **Evaluate the input**

Remind learners to keep their objectives in mind throughout the training intervention and to speak to the trainer if their needs are not being met. If the training is provided by an external organisation, ask the learners to give you their reactions to the course at a debriefing session on their return. Encourage them to be honest in their opinion of the value and relevance of the training.

6 Assess the application of training and learning in the workplace

This aspect has traditionally been the most neglected, and Kirkpatrick's research suggests that lack of application in the workplace is a major reason for the failure of training. The process of evaluation involves comparing actual results with expectations. Encourage learners to produce realistic action plans for implementing what they have learned once they are back at work. In the longer term, perhaps in three months, ask the learners what the training has helped them achieve and what they now perceive to be the benefits of the training they received. The answer could be, for example, that the knowledge gained has contributed to a successful business plan.

7 Use the results

The information gained from evaluation is critical in starting the training cycle over again and planning what needs to be tackled next year, and how. Evaluation sets out key facts and measures of progress more clearly than any sort of gut reaction or guesswork.

As a manager you should avoid:

- failing to set indicators for activities that are hard to measure – if the best available is rough and ready, it remains the best available and is still better than nothing
- trying to justify poor results with excuses – if there is a lesson to be learned, make the most of it
- relying exclusively on 'happy sheets'
- giving up – evaluating training is widely regarded as the most difficult aspect of the training function.

Peter Senge
The learning organisation

Introduction

Peter Senge (b. 1947) is chairman of the Society for Organizational Learning, a non-profit, member-governed organisation based in Massachusetts. He graduated in engineering from Stanford before doing a PhD on social systems modelling at MIT. For many years Senge has studied how firms and organisations develop adaptive capabilities in a world of increasing complexity and change, but the success of his book *The Fifth Discipline* popularised the concept of the 'learning organisation'.

Published in 1990, *The Fifth Discipline* brought the world's attention to this rather unassuming man, who suddenly found himself the modern equivalent of a medieval crusader seeking against the odds to dramatically change corporate America, and indeed the rest of the world. His message is simple: the learning organisation values and believes that competitive advantage derives from continued learning, both individual and collective. Further, the new challenges of the information age demand that not only businesses, but also educational institutions and governments, radically transform themselves. Senge describes himself as an 'idealistic pragmatist' and spends much time helping leaders of companies, education and government to build learning organisations.

In 1999 Senge was named by the *Journal of Business Strategy* as one of the twenty-four people who have had the greatest influence on business strategy over the past 100 years.

The Fifth Discipline

In *The Fifth Discipline* Senge suggests that there are five basic ingredients for a learning organisation.

1 Systems thinking. Senge's approach to organisations is a 'systems' approach that views the organisation as a living entity, with its own behaviour and learning patterns. He introduces the idea of 'systems archetypes' to help managers spot repetitive patterns leading to recurrent problems or limits to growth.

2 Personal mastery. Every modern manager recognises the importance of developing skills and competencies in individuals, but Senge takes this notion further by stressing the importance of spiritual growth in the learning organisation. True spiritual growth exposes us to a deeper reality; it helps us learn how to see the current reality more clearly and by highlighting the difference between vision and the current reality generates a creative tension, out of which successful learning arises.

Senge believes that a learning organisation is 'a group of people who are continually enhancing their capability to create their future' by 'changing individuals so that they produce results they care about, accomplish things that are important to them'.

3 Mental models. The systems approach is continued with Senge's emphasis on mental models. This discipline requires managers to construct mental models for the driving forces behind the organisation's values and principles. Senge alerts his readers to the impact of acquired patterns of thinking at the organisational level and the need to develop non-defensive mechanisms for examining the nature of these patterns.

4 Shared vision. According to Senge, true creativity and innovation are based on group creativity, and the shared vision the group depends on can only be built on the personal vision of its members. He claims that shared vision occurs when the vision is no longer seen by the team members as separate from the self.

5 Team learning. Effective team learning involves alternating processes for dialogue and discussion. Dialogue is exploratory and widens possibilities, whereas discussion narrows down the options to find the best alternatives for future decisions. Although these two processes are complementary, they need to be separated; sadly, most teams lack the ability to distinguish between these two modes and to move consciously between them.

Senge's basic premise is simple: people should put aside their old ways of thinking (mental models), learn to be open with others (personal mastery), understand how the company really works (systems thinking), form a plan everyone can agree on (shared vision) and then work together to achieve that vision (team learning).

Practical tools: *The Fifth Discipline Fieldbook*

Recognising that the ideas contained in *The Fifth Discipline* needed to be made more accessible to practising managers, Senge and his colleagues produced a more practical guide, *The Fifth Discipline Fieldbook*. Throughout the book, the authors stress that anyone who wants to be part of a learning organisation must go through a personal change and must be willing to do so. To help this process, Senge and his co-authors provide a set of elaborate personal awareness exercises. The fieldbook was designed as a resource for dipping into and contains many good ideas and case studies. Even if you find Senge's thinking too general, it is well worth scrutinising for references and new ideas. Here are just a few:

● **System archetypes and causal loops.** The fieldbook devotes a lot of time to mapping processes in organisations, analysing feedback loops and identifying typical organisational problems (the system archetypes). This process-mapping tool can help employees to work out how complex systems interact and to develop their 'mental models' of the organisation. The 'Beer Game' described in *The Fifth Discipline* is a simulation based on these models.

- **Left- and right-hand columns.** By writing down in meetings what you really think (left-hand column) and what you actually said (right-hand column), you can analyse and identify personal prejudices that get in the way of really productive work.
- **The ladder of inference.** This exercise provides a step model for analysing our values, beliefs and actions. Climbing down the ladder helps us to discover why we behave the way we do and helps us to avoid jumping to dangerous conclusions. The steps on the ladder are as follows:

  - I take ACTIONS based on my beliefs
  - I adopt BELIEFS about the world
  - I draw CONCLUSIONS
  - I make ASSUMPTIONS based on the meanings added to my mental models
  - I add MEANINGS (cultural and personal)
  - I select DATA from what I observe
  - I OBSERVE data and experiences.

- **The container.** This is a dialogue tool that has proved highly effective (if not explosive) in some organisations. People at a meeting are encouraged to imagine a container that holds everyone's hostile thoughts and feelings. As everyone speaks out, putting their fears, prejudices and anger on the table, the hostility between different factions is neutralised, because it is exposed in a safe place for all to discuss. In the early days of such experiments, a good facilitator is probably essential.
- **Learning labs and flight simulators.** The fieldbook provides useful references for those who wish to design effective simulations for training sessions.

In perspective

Though *The Fifth Discipline* was a bestseller, its basic concepts had emerged from extensive research carried out at the influential Sloan School of Management at MIT over 15 years. The success of the learning organisation concept is a reflection of the times.

None of *The Fifth Discipline*'s concepts are new, but Senge was able to put them all together and create a simple but powerful concept.

Senge is a product of his age, probably greatly influenced by the culture of the 1960s in the US. His systems approach towards organisations shows the same maturity displayed in the systems analysis tools developed by people like Peter Checkland at Lancaster University. Here the organisation is viewed as a 'superorganism' with its own behaviour patterns, but also profoundly influenced by the value and nature of its constituent members. The sad fact is that Senge was one of the first management gurus to make the accepted beliefs of a whole generation of social scientists, biologists and environmentalists credible to the corporate world. Senge says:

We live under a massive illusion of separation from one another, from nature, from the universe, from everything. We're depleting the earth and we're fragmenting our spirit. The symptoms are pollution, anger and fear. Everything in our culture is about the management of impressions and appearances, from physical fitness to the way we dress. And yet on another level we know it's all bullshit.

Today, there is little evidence that the change in attitude needed to achieve Senge's ideal of long-term corporate sustainability and freedom for all to achieve personal mastery is in sight, as there are few organisations that have been able to implement his ideas successfully.

The main criticism of Senge's work is the inherent difficulty of applying these models. Senge was trained as an engineer and then became involved in social research. Both require a systems approach, but this isn't easy to learn. A thorough grasp of systems thinking is not something which can be acquired at a three-day seminar on the subject. Nor can most companies afford the luxury of their top executives learning to 'crash land' for too long.

Breaking old corporate habits is hard. Transforming an enterprise into a learning organisation is highly problematical and not for the faint-hearted. The reason for this is simple: to move forward to a new, cooperative learning model, managers have to give up their traditional areas of power and control. They have to hand over power to the learners and allow them to make mistakes. In a blame-oriented culture, this change in attitude remains a major obstacle.

Despite its drawbacks, *The Fifth Discipline* has proved highly influential. Although it represents an elusive ideal for most corporate cultures, the concept has stimulated debate about and acceptance of issues such as self-managed development, empowerment and creativity. Its practical impact can be seen in modern human resources management strategies, teamwork principles and quality models.

It is more important perhaps to recognise that in life all the most profound truths are deceptively simple, yet almost impossible to apply in practice. The difficulty experienced in applying Senge's ideas does not invalidate them; if anything it confirms their importance for companies in the next millennium.

Developing a mentoring scheme

Mentoring is a relationship in which one person (the mentor), who is usually someone more experienced and often more senior, helps another (the mentee) to discover more about themselves, their potential and their capabilities.

Mentoring should not be seen as an additional or supplementary management task, but as part of a style and an approach to management that puts the mentee's development at the heart of the business process.

The relationship between mentor and mentee can be informal, with the mentee relying on the mentor for guidance, support, help and feedback. It can also be a more formal arrangement between two people within an organisation who respect and trust each other, and who have organisational backing to develop the relationship and seek positive outcomes from it. This checklist focuses on formal, organisational schemes.

Mentoring can be used as a developmental approach, and helps to demonstrate organisational commitment to the individual's development in a non-dictatorial way. It can also be highly effective, providing in the mentor an organisation-backed, uninvolved party who can guide, advise and listen to the mentee, in full confidentiality – and it complements other forms of learning and development.

Care should be taken, however, as unstructured or informal mentoring can sometimes be seen as patronage, giving the mentee an unfair advantage.

This checklist describes the steps and considerations involved in developing an organisational mentoring scheme.

Action checklist

1 Check the organisational culture

For a mentoring scheme to be successful, a suitable organisational culture needs to be in place. Check for:

- a clear and accepted vision of where the organisation is going
- the promotion of learning and development activities among employees
- levels of cooperation and support between different sections of the organisation
- a climate of trust throughout the organisation.

The key to success is trust. If this is lacking, a programme of change may be needed before an organisation-wide mentoring scheme can be attempted with any hope of success.

2 Establish the goals of the scheme

Consider why you need to establish a mentoring scheme. Common reasons include:

- to improve and maintain the skills and morale of employees
- to provide an additional source of guidance and support beyond that offered by line managers
- to enable employees to realise ambitious career development plans
- to improve internal communications.

3 Obtain the commitment and support of senior management

A mentoring scheme that does not have the visible support of senior management will almost certainly fail. Without this support, employees will feel that the scheme is under-resourced, and that there is no authority behind it to progress any recommended development activities. With senior management commitment, however, confidence will cascade down to mentors and mentees, who will be more likely to give their time, commitment and energy to the scheme.

4 Find a champion

Appoint a mentoring champion who is a senior member of the organisation (possibly the person selected to manage the scheme). Ensure that the person is seen to be actively supportive on a day-to-day basis. This will be demonstrated through their:

- help in developing the scheme
- willingness to contribute to it themselves by mentoring others
- involvement with others participating in the scheme
- commitment to training for those participating in the scheme.

5 Establish terms of reference

- **Clear up 'advice and advise' in a legal sense.** Ownership of the mentoring process is with the individual mentee. By adopting a joint agreement on a course of action, the mentor should not put themselves in the position of offering legal advice or guidance which could make them liable for the outcomes. Establish the difference between mentoring and eliciting and agreeing action, making the pros and cons clear, and offering advice.

- **Distinguish mentoring from coaching.** It is generally accepted that mentoring is distinct from coaching. Coaching is usually carried out as part of a paid job with objectives, involves a teaching aspect and should be impartial. Mentoring, by contrast, is usually conducted by a self-selected volunteer who is personally involved, aims to facilitate rather than direct a mentee's development and works with no particular personal agenda.

- **Confidentiality.** All discussions between the mentor and mentee should be strictly confidential. The only exception to this is if the mentee agrees that the content can be relayed to a third party (such as a line manager).

● **Target audience.** Establish who the scheme is aimed at.

6 Start small

Begin with a pilot scheme. It is unrealistic to expect everything to be perfect the first time, so testing is needed. A pilot will limit blunders to a core sample of identifiable and responsible volunteer mentors who have a strong interest in developing others on a personal basis. The result will be a more reliable, consistent and robust mentoring process.

7 Identify and train the mentors

Mentoring should be a voluntary activity, so issue a general invitation to employees to attract those who wish to become mentors. It is important, however, to establish a selection process to ensure the quality of those who mentor others.

Training is also important for mentors, who must be fully conversant with the mentoring scheme and what is or is not 'acceptable'. Mentors will need to have a clear understanding of:

● the mentoring process

● the difference between mentoring and directing

● the boundaries of mentoring (for example, psychological counselling goes beyond these boundaries)

● the skills necessary for effective mentoring.

8 Identify problems in advance

Work out what you are going to do if and when any of the following occur:

● conflict between the aims of the scheme and 'hidden agendas'

● a relational breakdown between mentor and mentee

● disruption to patterns of development through new tasks or responsibilities

- obstructive behaviour from the line manager.

9 Work out the logistics

Make sure you have arrangements in place for:

- announcements, promotion and awareness of the scheme
- questions, problems and reassurance
- the process of pairing mentors and mentees
- setting a framework for the first meeting.

10 Establish evaluation procedures

Plan to review the scheme on an annual basis against:

- the goals stated at the introduction of the scheme
- the success or failure of mentoring relationships, identifying the reasons behind both.

Make sure you include feedback from mentees, as this will be essential input for amending or improving the scheme.

As a manager you should avoid:

- making assumptions on the basis of early successes or failures – each mentee will have different obstacles to overcome
- forgetting that all participants are volunteers – directiveness is not on the menu.

Working with your
HR department

In most organisations, people are the biggest single item of cost, the biggest source of value and the biggest source of risk. Understanding the links between people management and business performance provides valuable business intelligence, and in a growing number of organisations the human resources (HR) function and the rest of the business work together to develop these.

In large organisations there may be a number of HR departments serving different business populations and including both specialist (focusing on areas such as recruitment, compensation, training) and generalist HR professionals at different levels of seniority and experience. Smaller organisations are less likely to have this level of specialisation, and, indeed, in many small companies HR may well be carried out by a manager with additional responsibilities. There is also a growing trend towards outsourcing HR functions. This checklist assumes a dedicated, in-house HR function, but the guidelines can be adapted to suit other situations.

This checklist aims to help line managers in organisations which have a dedicated in-house HR function to develop productive working relationships with the department and get the most benefit and value from the services they provide. Many HR departments are now developing strategic roles within the business and there is a move towards increasing the role of line managers in people management activities. The time and effort involved in developing effective relationships and working in cooperation with your HR department can produce significant benefits including:

- opportunities to understand better the links between recruitment, people management, reward and so on, and their impact on the business
- support and help in recruiting, retaining, managing and developing your team
- early warning of potential people and organisational problems, which might otherwise cause disruption and involve unexpected costs
- a guide to the legal minefield of employment issues
- a more effective service – HR personnel will be better able to gauge and meet your needs
- a more efficient service, especially in terms of accuracy and timeliness
- a sounding-board for your plans and ideas
- support for your own development.

Action checklist

1 Consider what you want from your HR department

HR spans a number of functions:

- transaction processor – the classic nuts-and-bolts service
- technical expert – in employment and management best practice
- employee advocate – helping you take account of the employee's perspective
- strategic partner – an integral part of, and contributor to, your management team.

2 Make the most of HR as transaction processor

HR transactional functions may include:

- ensuring that employee policies and procedures are kept up-to-date and legally compliant, and are correctly implemented

- administering and managing recruitment, including receiving and sifting applications, arranging interviews and other assessment processes, preparing contracts, checking references and ensuring the legality of the employment

- administering changes to terms and conditions

- managing employee benefits

- keeping records and employee information in paper and electronic formats

- tracking absence (holidays and sickness)

- developing and running induction and training events

- managing the processes through which people leave the organisation, including termination payments, exit interviews and return of company property

- running the payroll in some companies.

For a timely, efficient service:

- provide HR with all necessary information in good time. Forms often seem overly bureaucratic, but they are usually the easiest way of capturing information. Even if you keep your own employee files for colleagues reporting directly to you, HR files are a useful back-up, especially as individuals have the right to see all information about themselves

- make sure you know how to use the HR information system if you and your staff have access to it

- keep copies of information you provide to HR, especially information needed for the day-to-day management of your employees – performance appraisal records and job descriptions, for example. Ensure that 'private' files do not hold inappropriate information, such as notes which could be misinterpreted and lead to costly tribunal claims

- agree with HR what level of service you need – with regard to response times, for example. You may even wish to draw up a service level agreement. But be aware that you are only one of the HR department's customers and that a slower, accurate service may be better than an overhasty one

● do query bureaucracy if it is hindering you from carrying out your own job – HR is there to support you. There may be good reasons such as legal compliance for the complexity or detail required, but equally, some of the processes may need pruning

● talk to HR if you or your team are not satisfied with the service you are receiving and work with them to get the service you need.

3 Make the most of HR as technical expert

HR technical expertise may cover:

● employment law

● individual behaviour

● performance management

● compensation

● employment relations

● organisational behaviour

● resourcing

● training and development.

Treat HR personnel as you would any other experts or consultants. It is tempting to think that managing and employing people is just common sense, and in many ways it is – acting 'reasonably' is the core of all management and employment good practice. But employee expectations are rising and management techniques are becoming more sophisticated. In both the UK and the EU, employment law is now a specialised discipline and mistakes can be expensive for the company and for individual managers, who may carry personal legal liability for some of their actions.

To get most benefit from HR's technical expertise:

- give the HR department all the information it needs to advise you
- don't waste your own time second-guessing the department – question and challenge, but also listen to HR professionals and trust their knowledge, even if their advice is unpalatable
- use their expertise before turning to expensive external advice from consultants, but accept that in some areas they may want a second opinion themselves
- be aware that they need training to develop and maintain their professional competence.

4 Make the most of HR as employee advocate

HR's employee advocate functions include acting as:

- a release valve
- a conduit of information up and down the organisation
- an early warning system for organisational problems
- a management conscience
- an objective facilitator helping to resolve disciplinary or grievance situations
- a negotiator, sometimes in conflict situations or relations with trade unions
- a mediator.

This is more than a 'welfare' role – HR people should have the exposure and credibility, with both employees and managers, to play an effective part in maintaining good employee relations. This can mean that they are in a difficult situation, representing on the one hand, the views of employees to management, and on the other hand, the views of management to employees. To walk this tightrope successfully, they need the trust of both employees and managers. To facilitate this:

- don't allow the HR department to be viewed as distant and remote
- don't be suspicious of conversations between your employees and HR staff

- trust your HR people and accept that they may not tell you everything – confidentiality is critical in maintaining trust

- listen to what HR people say and also to what they do not say – this can be a subtle way of giving you a hint without breaching confidentiality

- use them to disseminate information formally and through the grapevine

- consult them on any people issues before a crisis develops

- encourage them in developing their counselling, negotiation and facilitation skills.

5 Make the most of HR as strategic partner

HR strategic partner functions may include:

- acting as part of the management team

- providing a people management framework and strategy to support the business plan

- providing a 'people' perspective for business planning activities

- providing a 'people' perspective for management decision-making

- acting as a driver for culture change

- facilitating organisation and team development

- driving the development of people to ensure robust succession management strategies

- acting as management coaches and mentors

- acting as devil's advocate.

These activities should never be outsourced, as they are key to the success of the business. The phrase 'strategic partner' may appear to be the latest management buzzword, but it conveys both the level and the manner in which HR should operate to give you value for money.

To get the greatest benefit from your HR service:

- keep your HR people fully informed, and involve them in your plans and decisions
- expect them to contribute fully in management meetings, not just on HR issues
- use them as a sounding-board for the early development of your ideas
- use them as your own management coach or mentor
- encourage them to develop their business knowledge.

6 Measure HR's contribution to your operations

Here are some examples of measures available.

Human capital accounting

This is a current preoccupation in business and may become a requirement for company accounts in the future. Putting numbers on the cost of employing people is comparatively easy; it is far more difficult to put numbers on the 'value' of people. However, your people are likely to be one of your most expensive assets, so it is worth looking for ways of measuring the value you gain from them. Some elements you may want to consider are:

- cost – pay and benefits (including social charges); expenses; occupancy costs; IT equipment and systems costs; training; labour turnover; absenteeism; employee litigation
- value – company performance (sales, profits) as a factor of total employment costs; improvement in company performance as a factor of training or systems costs.

'People' key performance indicators

These can be compared with results in previous years, budgets and targets, or local and industry benchmarks. They may include:

- training and development days and costs (not just formal courses, but all days spent on development activities)
- labour turnover or employee retention

- reasons for people leaving
- number of vacancies filled internally
- time taken to recruit replacements – this may be an indicator of your HR function's efficiency, or of your company's attractiveness as an employer
- sickness absenteeism (short-term, long-term)
- numbers of formal disciplinary/grievance incidents
- responses to employee attitude surveys
- performance appraisal ratings (and number of performance appraisals held)
- employee contributions to suggestion schemes and process improvement programmes
- customer satisfaction survey responses
- impact of workforce optimisation on sales growth
- labour turnover correlating with sales
- leadership performance as a predictor of growth on return of capital employed.

The most useful indicators are often developed in collaboration between the HR function and others. If your HR department is not able to produce these, the initiative can begin with another department, such as finance, given that people are usually the biggest single item of cost.

HR service level agreements

These may typically cover:

- descriptions of services, activities and deliverables to be provided by HR
- performance measures for each of these
- descriptions of HR and business management roles and responsibilities, and communication mechanisms
- performance reporting mechanisms

- mechanisms for resolving any issues
- costs and resources.

Most of these measures are gauges of your own success, but they also assess HR's contribution and the extent to which HR truly is your strategic partner.

As a manager you should avoid:

- trying to duplicate the activities or second-guess the advice of HR personnel
- accepting without question procedural requirements which are overly rigid or bureaucratic, or which interfere with the achievement of your business goals.

The psychological contract

The psychological contract refers to the set of expectations that exist between you and your employer. It is most easily defined as 'the set of unwritten expectations that exist between an individual employee and the organisation'. All employees have some form of psychological contract, which underpins the relationships that are hard to define clearly in a formal employment contract. This can cover:

- knowledge and skills development
- your work and motivation
- relationships with your bosses and co-workers
- the role that you are expected to fulfil
- ethics – the ethical code by which you and the organisation will act
- the support that you can expect from the organisation and vice versa.

The psychological contract is about unspoken and tacit expectations between the employee and employer, rather than formal agreements. An agreement can only be reached if unspoken expectations are made explicit and accepted by both sides.

The psychological contract is a subtle relationship made up of many factors. It is often considered a key factor in understanding employment relationships, as disappointed expectations can make a big impact upon employee relations. A psychological contract, because it is implicit rather than explicit, can shift over time, and is subject to internal and external changes of all kinds. This checklist focuses on understanding the unspoken expectations and perceptions that you and your employer may have, evaluating the degree to which these fit with your requirements, and possibly seeking to clarify or change them, if necessary.

Action checklist

1 Negotiate your psychological contract from the start

The psychological contract is first explored at the job interview. The organisation assesses how you might behave in your role and how you would fit in. This will give you an early opportunity to judge whether you would be comfortable working in the company. It will form the basis of the understandings you will have with the people with whom you work – colleagues, business partners and customers.

Think carefully about the organisational culture being presented and the type of people with whom you will work. If their values and expectations initially appear questionable, it may be because you are seeing these as unfair or unsuitable to you.

A simple psychological contract exercise that can be used in interviews or appraisals consists of four simple questions:

- What do you expect from the organisation?
- What does the organisation expect of you?
- What do you give the organisation?
- What does the organisation give you?

2 Obtain more information about the organisation's culture and values

During the first few weeks in a job, your psychological contract will develop rapidly as you gather information about others' values and expectations. Watching when, where, why and how colleagues speak and act is a good way to assess the realities of the organisation's behaviour. Don't be afraid to test your understanding by gently pushing against boundaries, or asking questions.

3 Compare the organisation's policies with your psychological contract

The two should be complementary, not mutually exclusive. You need to check that what is explicit is the same as what you have implicitly understood or assumed. For example, are employees really consulted about change? Are statements about quality and customer service actually lived up to? Basic, general questions might include: 'Do they do what they say?' or 'Do they say one thing but expect another?'

If the answers to these questions seem unsatisfactory, then you may need to reconsider your future with the organisation.

4 Examine the psychological contract

Psychological contracts have many elements. Among the most important are:

- **Knowledge and experience.** What are the expectations about what I know and can do, and how I use my knowledge and skills? How will I be helped to improve my skills? How am I expected to share skills and knowledge – formally (for example, reports) or informally (for example, at team meetings)?

- **Motivation.** What are my real motivations for this job and how do these affect my performance? What motivates the people around me and how can knowledge of this improve my job? What are the rewards and disadvantages of working here?

- **Goals (and means).** How do things happen in the organisation? Is the rulebook closely followed or simply ignored? Who do I go through to get things done? What happens if I don't follow the expected channels? Would I be happy with this?

- **Role.** Who do I want to be in the organisation? What is the real nature and content of the job? How do I avoid being a figurehead and get taken seriously? What are people's emotional expectations of me that weren't communicated at the start?

- **Ethics.** What are the moral principles that guide the organisation? Am I happy with these? Are any laws being broken? What morals and principles must I exhibit when dealing with others (including customers and outside agencies)?

5 Review the psychological contract

A psychological contract is a description of how well you fit into the organisation and how well the organisation suits you. If both you and the organisation agree on your role, what is expected of you and what you expect of the organisation, there is a good fit.

But the situation may change over time. The business environment never stands still; people move on; the type of work changes; or the company adopts a new strategy and implements new policies and practices. You may react negatively to such changes. To deal with this, consider the various elements of your working life to identify where the problems are.

- **Your boss.** Have your boss's expectations of you, your role and your workload changed? Are you unhappy with his or her way of allocating work to you or communicating with you? Do you have too many bosses?

- **Your co-workers.** Do you feel sidelined or left out? Are you happy with the work of others? Do they have personalities different from your own that seem to be valued more highly?

- **The physical environment.** Is it unsafe, overcrowded or otherwise unsatisfactory?

- **Your work.** Are you either bored or overworked? Do you have too much spare time? Have you increased your expertise or knowledge, without improving the quality of your output? Are you frustrated because you can't change something you think needs changing?

- **Your private life.** Is something at work affecting your private life or vice versa?

6 Resolve tensions in the psychological contract

Be honest with yourself and decide what it is you now want from your work. If possible, clarify your understanding of the existing psychological contract to reduce any obvious areas of tension or conflict.

Check out your psychological contract to resolve:

- who can help you deal with your concerns, and how both the people and the problems should be approached
- how the organisation expects problems to be recognised and dealt with.

As a manager you should avoid:

- neglecting your psychological contract, or failing to establish your understanding of expectations where possible
- being too rigid in your opinions, or in how you work with others
- expecting everyone to share your expectations and values
- assuming that people will always hold the same expectations of you and your role
- relying on expectations based only on first impressions.

Understanding organisational culture

Organisational culture is the way that things are done in an organisation, the unwritten rules that influence individual and group behaviour and attitudes. Organisational culture is defined by the organisation's structure, the behaviour and attitudes of its employees, and the management and leadership style adopted by its managers.

Organisational culture is the personality and character of the organisation and is composed of the values, beliefs and basic assumptions that are shared by members of an organisation.

An understanding of organisational culture is crucial for effective leadership. Leaders and managers will be better placed to implement strategy and achieve their goals if they understand the culture of their organisation. Strategies that are inconsistent with organisational culture are more likely to fail, while strategies that are in line with it are more likely to succeed. It is also important to understand the existing culture of an organisation before thinking about change.

The workforce of an organisation swiftly comes to understand its particular culture. Culture is a concept that may be difficult to express plainly, but everyone knows it when they see it. For example, the culture of an informal software company may be quite different from that of a large financial corporation, and different again from that of a hospital or a university.

To gain an understanding of the culture of an organisation, the relationships between values, behaviours and unwritten rules must be examined. This checklist outlines the main steps to take and questions to ask to help gain this understanding. Some well-known methods used to classify organisational culture are also introduced.

Action checklist

Organisations are human communities, peopled with individuals. Once managers develop an understanding of why people and their organisation behave as they do they will be more able to improve communication, organisation, control, effectiveness and ultimately, results.

An understanding of an organisation's culture can be gained by:

1 Reading

For example:

- the mission statement, in which the organisation's goals and values are explicitly stated
- publications, reports and newsletters – consider what is mentioned, emphasised or omitted and how the organisation presents itself
- the organisation's website and intranet.

2 Talking to people who work in the organisation

Ask them:

- for their impressions of the organisation
- what words they would use to describe the organisation (for example, professional, experienced, friendly, stable, secure)
- what sorts of behaviours are expected of employees
- whether the message they get about the culture is consistent across all levels and units within the organisation.

3 Observing the physical environment

- Do the furnishings and decor make a particular statement?
- Are the surroundings formal or informal?
- How do people dress – do they dress differently depending on their position within the organisation?

4 Assessing communication styles

- How do staff communicate with one another (face-to-face, phone, email)?
- How do people address one another in the organisation, and how are superiors addressed?
- If a manager's office door is closed, how do people react and approach the individual?
- How accessible or approachable are senior managers?
- How are organisational decisions communicated to employees?
- Is feedback (positive or negative) given regularly?

5 Looking at the nature of decision-making and the impact on stakeholders

- How are HR policies such as remuneration implemented in practice?
- What level of priority and attention is given to customer service levels, and how are customer concerns or complaints handled?
- How are statutory regulations being applied?
- How is the balance between customer and business benefit handled when specifying products?
- How are profit and loss accounts and the balance sheet managed?

6 Considering timekeeping

- Does the organisation operate with fixed working hours?

- What time do people come to work and do they arrive on time?
- Are coffee or tea breaks taken? Do they become extended breaks?
- Do people work their set hours only or do they stay late?

7 Analysing groups and networks

- Do people seem to prefer working in groups or individually?
- Do people gather together at lunch?
- Do people socialise at work, or outside the workplace?
- Do subcultures exist within departments or within professional groups?
- Are people encouraged to work beyond their own department or does a silo mentality prevail?

8 Observing dress codes

- Do people dress formally or informally?
- Are there dress-down days?
- How do people dress for special appointments or meetings?

9 Monitoring meetings

- Does everyone participate in meetings?
- Are people encouraged to share ideas at meetings?
- Who speaks at meetings?
- What do people say if they arrive late for a meeting?

10 Considering organisational boundaries

- What types of positions do women and members of minority groups hold in the organisation?
- Is face-saving important to people?
- Does the organisation have a sense of stability, or is there relentless change?

- Is there a common shared language consisting of jargon and acronyms?
- How are new employees inducted and integrated?

As a manager you should avoid:

- assuming that an organisation's culture can be fully understood through superficial observation
- believing that the values expressed, for example, in mission statements necessarily reflect the values actually practised by the organisation.

Some methods used to classify organisational culture

A number of management thinkers have studied organisational culture and attempted to classify different types of culture. The following approaches may be helpful in assessing and understanding the culture of an organisation.

Edgar Schein

Schein believed that culture is the most difficult organisational attribute to change and that it can outlast products, services, founders and leaders. His model looks at culture from the standpoint of the observer and describes organisational culture at three levels:

- organisational attributes that can be seen, felt and heard by the uninitiated observer, including the facilities, offices, decor, furnishings and dress, and how people visibly interact with others and with organisational outsiders
- the professed culture of an organisation's members – company slogans, mission statements and other operational creeds are useful examples
- the organisation's implied assumptions, which are unseen and

not consciously identified in everyday interactions between organisational members. Even people with the experience to understand this deepest level of organisational culture can become accustomed to its attributes, reinforcing the invisibility of its existence.

Geert Hofstede

Hofstede explored the national and regional cultural influences that affect the behaviour of organisations. He identified five dimensions of culture in his study of national influences:

- **Power distance** – the extent to which the less powerful members of organisations accept and expect the unequal distribution of power. This suggests that a society's level of inequality is endorsed by the followers as much as by the leaders

- **Uncertainty avoidance** – reflects the extent to which a society tolerates uncertainty, risk and ambiguity

- **Individualism versus collectivism** – the extent to which people are expected to act as individuals, or as members of the group or organisation

- **Masculinity versus femininity** – the value placed on traditionally male or female values

- **Long-term versus short-term orientation** – in societies that focus on the long term, thrift and perseverance are valued more highly than in societies that focus on the short term, where respect for tradition and the reciprocation of gifts and favours are more highly valued.

Charles Handy

Handy links organisational structure to organisational culture. He describes:

- **Power culture** – power is concentrated among a few with control spreading from the centre. Power cultures have few rules and little bureaucracy; decision-making can be swift

- **Role culture** – authority is clearly delegated within a highly defined structure. Such organisations typically form hierarchical bureaucracies where power derives from a person's position and little opportunity exists for expert power

- **Task culture** – teams are formed to solve particular problems with power deriving from expertise
- **Person culture** – all individuals believe themselves superior to the organisation. The concept of an organisation suggests that a group of like-minded individuals pursues organisational goals. For this type of organisation, survival can become difficult.

Gerry Johnson and Kevan Scholes

Johnson and Scholes developed the cultural web in 1992. It is a representation of assumptions that are taken for granted by an organisation. This helps management focus on the key factors of culture and their impact on strategic issues. It can identify blockages to and facilitators of change to improve performance and competitive advantage.

The cultural web contains six interrelated elements:

- **Stories** – the past and present events and people talked about inside and outside an organisation
- **Rituals and routines** – the daily behaviour and actions of people that are regarded as acceptable
- **Symbols** – the visual representations of an organisation, including logos, office décor, and formal or informal dress codes
- **Organisational structure** – including structures defined by the organisation chart, and the unwritten lines of power and influence that indicate whose contributions are most valued
- **Control systems** – the ways that an organisation is controlled, including financial systems, quality systems and rewards
- **Power structures** – power in an organisation may lie with one or two executives, a group of executives, or a department. These people exert the strongest influence on decisions, operations and strategic direction.

Niccolò Machiavelli
The patron saint of power

Introduction

Throughout most of the five centuries since his death, Niccolò
Machiavelli has not been a popular figure. There have always
been a few people who appreciated his genius, but most have
so closely associated him with intrigue and dark deeds that the
term Machiavellian has entered almost every European language
– a word that means something very different from good
management. Fortunately, in the past 100 years or so, a more
reasoned view of his work has developed and the enormous
value of Machiavelli's philosophy, and its remarkable relevance to
modern society, has progressively emerged.

No one has done more to develop the comparisons between
Machiavelli's ideas and current management practice than Antony
Jay. In his now classic 1967 book, *Management and Machiavelli*,
Jay gives us a masterly interpretation of Machiavelli's philosophy
in twentieth-century terms. He then examines, with the eyes
of a historian and political scientist, how this philosophy has
influenced the development of management science and the
work of so many business practitioners and researchers.

Courageously, Jay takes on Peter Drucker and other management
thinkers who have marvelled at the rapid and unchallenged way
in which management science has emerged as a new institution
(even discipline) in the twentieth century, despite the absence
of a tenable theory of business practice. Jay sees this as no
miracle. While accepting that there may be no useful theory, he

believes there is a sound political theory of business enterprise.
He suggests:

*The new science of management is in fact only a continuation
of the old art of government, and when you study management
theory side by side with political theory, and the management
case studies side by side with political history, you realise that you
are only studying two very similar branches of the same subject.*

Once this relationship is accepted, the importance of Machiavelli,
the first great analyst of political theory, is firmly established.

Jay identifies Machiavelli's contribution to management science
precisely when he says:

*[H]owever marginal his relevance to academic historians,
[Machiavelli] is in fact bursting with urgent advice and acute
observations for top management of the greatest private and
public corporations all over the world. You only have to look for it.*

Life and career

Machiavelli was born in 1469, the son of a Florentine lawyer.
He first came to public notice when, in 1498, aged twenty-nine,
he was appointed secretary of the Second Chancery, part of
the complex bureaucracy that ran Florence as a city state. His
appointment came after the execution of Girolamo Savonarola, a
friar-politician who, after leading a revolt that expelled the Medicis
and established a democratic republic, dominated Florentine life
until he fell foul of the papacy and was burned for heresy.

Machiavelli held the post of secretary for fourteen years, during
which time his influence was significant. He took part in thirty
foreign missions, meeting most of Europe's leading politicians
and rulers. This opportunity to learn about government, politics
and economics must have been unique. Unfortunately, it was
not to last. In 1512 the Medicis returned to power and Machiavelli
lost his post immediately. He was then suspected, quite wrongly,

of plotting against the Medicis, for which he was arrested, imprisoned and tortured. Although eventually found innocent, he was expelled from Florence and forced to spend the rest of his life in exile on an isolated farm. His many attempts to re-enter political life failed and he died in 1527 still struggling to regain his lost influence.

Although Machiavelli may not have enjoyed his time in exile, the world has gained immeasurably from it. The enforced idleness allowed him to write prodigiously about his experiences and ideas. His written works include a history of Florence, several plays and two books that established him as a great authority on power politics: *The Prince* and *The Discourses*. Max Lerner, in his introduction to the 1950 Random House edition of *The Prince*, describes the book as 'a grammar of power'. There can be no more fitting description of this seminal work.

Key theories

Machiavelli presents no instant management theories, no clever techniques for solving day-to-day problems. He deals mainly with broad strategies, and to get value from his writing you need to interpret it and make comparisons. Perhaps the best approach is to first read Jay's introduction on the art of making such comparisons and then to read Machiavelli with a personal checklist of interests and questions.

The following examples show how certain passages in Machiavelli's writing bridge the seemingly huge gap between sixteenth-century politics and twentieth-century business.

• **Leadership.** Machiavelli provides several examples of good leaders and leaves his readers in no doubt about the importance of skilful leadership to the success of any enterprise. He dismisses luck and genius as the key to successful leadership and goes for 'shrewdness'. The dangers and risks a leader faces are dramatically illustrated (happily for us these are less terrifying today than in Renaissance Italy) and comparison is made between the relative ease in getting to a position of leadership and the difficult task of staying there.

● **Centralisation versus decentralisation.** Anyone who thinks that the problem of opting for centralised or decentralised control is a modern dilemma will be quickly persuaded otherwise by reading *The Prince*. Machiavelli's examples are drawn from strictly government and military events, but the comparisons with today's business world are easy to make. Perhaps his best advice comes when he is talking about the government of colonies and outposts. Poor communications in Renaissance times usually made decentralisation the only option in such cases, and Machiavelli's recommendations centre on what today we would call selection and training. The colonial governor must be carefully selected for his experience and loyalty, trained thoroughly in the state's way of doing things and made so familiar with 'best practice' that however isolated from 'head office' guidance he might be, the job will get done in a highly predictable way. Shades of William Whyte's *Organization Man*?

● **Takeovers.** The equivalent of a takeover in Machiavelli's world was the conquest of another country or the establishment of a colony. In such matters his advice is clear. The conqueror either totally subjugates the original inhabitants, so that rebellion is unlikely and the cost of garrisoning the place reduced to a minimum, or – and Machiavelli makes clear this is his preference – puts in a small team of 'key managers'. This team will displace only a small number of the original inhabitants, who being scattered cannot rebel, and the remainder will quickly toe the new management line since they have everything to gain from cooperation and a clear indication of what happens to those who do not cooperate. Parallels with business takeovers are frighteningly stark.

● **Change.** Machiavelli has little to offer in the way of ideas for coping with change, but shows clearly that the problems of introducing change were just as awesome and hazardous in the sixteenth century as they are today. In *The Prince* he says: 'It must be considered that there is nothing more difficult to carry out, nor more doubtful of success, nor more dangerous to handle, than to initiate a new order of things.'

● **Federations and bureaucracies.** Machiavelli compared the 'management' of sixteenth-century France and Turkey. He saw France as a 'federal organisation', a collection of independent baronies whose retainers regard their baron, and not the King, as the 'key manager'. Such organisations are difficult to control, impossible to change and the ruler is easily overthrown. Turkey, by contrast, was in Machiavelli's time a classic bureaucracy with a highly trained civil service. Civil servants were frequently moved around, hence they developed no local loyalties, and had a strict, hierarchical relationship with 'top management'. The ruler in such a state, being appointed by the 'system', is secure, respected and powerful. The comparison with today's large organisations needs little interpretation.

In perspective

The impact of Machiavelli's writing on politics has been accepted for some time, but the relevance of his ideas to business had to wait until the second half of the nineteenth century, when companies began to operate as large, complex organisations – the equivalent in Machiavelli's terms of a move from tribal society to corporate state. An English parson, writing in 1820, compares Machiavelli unfavourably with the devil, yet by the 1860s Victor Hugo was able to say: 'Machiavelli is not an evil genius, nor a cowardly writer, he is nothing but the fact ... not merely the Italian fact, he is the European fact.'

Machiavelli's image is not helped by what many see as an amoral attitude to power. It is easy to take offence when he unashamedly says: 'A prudent ruler ought not to keep faith when by so doing it would be against his interest, and when the reasons which made him bind himself no longer exist.'

Such statements are easier to accept if we remember that they were made in times very different from our own. They were also the words of a man who was a true observer; he reported what he saw and measured results dispassionately in terms of practical success or failure. He had moral views, as can be seen in his other writing, but on political issues he is a cold realist. He had, as Lerner so aptly observed, 'the clear-eyed capacity to distinguish between man as he ought to be and man as he actually is – between the ideal form of institutions and the pragmatic conditions under which they operate'.

By being so linked with intrigue, cruelty and opportunism, Machiavelli remains a man of his time. However, if we set him aside from the harsh realities of sixteenth-century Europe and look at how he observes human nature and organisations, we see a man who was centuries ahead of his time.

Employee engagement

There are many definitions of employee engagement. One simple definition cited by the McLeod report, *Engaging for Success*, commissioned by the UK government and published in July 2009, emphasises reciprocity for mutual benefit: 'When the business values the employee and the employee values the business.'

The McLeod report concludes that it is helpful to see employee engagement as

a workplace approach designed to ensure that employees are committed to their organisation's goals and values, motivated to contribute to organisational success, and are able at the same time to enhance their own sense of well-being.

This definition focuses on the employee's sense of purpose and energy directed towards organisational goals. By comparison with the more traditional but related term 'employee commitment', the emphasis is not just on a commitment to do one's job faithfully and effectively, but on an active and/or proactive engagement with the overall organisational aims and objectives which may involve 'going the extra mile' (or giving the 'discretionary performance' mentioned below). This involves a willingness to:

- go beyond individual job roles to assist colleagues or customers
- take advantage of new opportunities
- adapt readily to new circumstances
- make suggestions for improvements

- put forward new ideas.

Interest in the concept of employee engagement has been growing in recent years and this has been reinforced by the pressures of economic recession. Employers may have fewer skilled staff available and be working in situations where there is virtually no slack in the system. This makes it all the more important to make the best possible use of employees' skills and experience and to keep them happy – the loss of any individual may become critical, making it increasingly difficult to achieve business objectives.

Research findings have confirmed that employees who are satisfied and positively engaged in their work perform better and are more productive. A study carried out by Gallup, a research-based performance management consulting company, in 2006 found that the earnings per share growth rate of organisations with the highest engagement scores was two-and-a-half times that of organisations with the lowest levels of employee engagement. Organisations where employees showed high levels of engagement also demonstrated a greater capacity for innovation and experienced higher retention rates, less absenteeism and fewer work-related accidents. The McLeod report also highlighted the importance of employee engagement, identifying and illustrating significant improvements in a wide range of business performance indicators from studies of a cross-section of organisations. This work was extended in 2011 with the creation of a government employee engagement task force, chaired by David MacLeod and Nita Clarke, the report's authors.

For the organisation, employee engagement can be a valuable source of competitive advantage. It can improve performance, release innovation and creativity, lead to high levels of customer service, facilitate the management of change, increase staff retention levels and boost interest in training and development.

For the individual, engagement provides a sense of satisfaction in work, a feeling of belonging, and the opportunity to develop and use personal skills and abilities to make a contribution that is valued and appreciated,

When applied to those in leadership and management roles, engagement can also be taken to encompass the degree to which they have 'bought in' to the vision, mission, values and strategic intentions of the organisation. The MacLeod report, as well as several other studies, indicates that the release of the 'discretionary performance' of managers and staff (that is, the performance capability and commitment that is not utilised or even withheld due to lack of engagement and motivation) can add as much as 40% to productivity, making it one of the most significant sources of performance improvement available to an organisation.

Action checklist

1 Review the current situation

Start by assessing the current climate in the organisation, identifying areas of strength and weakness and uncovering things that are acting as barriers to engagement and need to be addressed. Many organisations choose to do this by means of an employee survey. This option can be expensive and time-consuming and requires careful consideration. The commitment of senior management is essential, both to provide the resources required and to take action on the findings. Resources will be needed for the selection or development of a suitable survey, the conduct of the survey and the implementation of any improvements found to be necessary – increases in training budgets, for example. It is also crucial to communicate clearly with employees about the aims and purpose of the survey, to ensure confidentiality and to assure employees that their views will be taken seriously. Without a clear commitment on the part of the employer to act on the results, a survey could be counter-productive. Nonetheless, an employee survey can give a clear indication of levels of engagement.

Other methods for gathering information include:

- employee focus groups
- exit interviews with employees leaving the organisation
- well-being audits.

Regular tracking of staff turnover, absence rates and grievances can also help to identify patterns and trends and to gauge current levels of engagement. When assessing levels of employee engagement, the work of psychologist Frederick Herzberg may be helpful. Herzberg identified drivers of workplace motivation which he called 'motivators' and 'hygiene factors' such as a comfortable working environment which, while they don't actually motivate employees, can prevent job dissatisfaction.

2 Develop a tailored organisational strategy

Employee engagement programmes may encompass a wide range of initiatives. Research has suggested that the best results are achieved with programmes that are tailored to an organisation and its employees. You may need to consider the needs and motivations of different groups of employees – older workers, younger workers, or disabled workers, for example. When drawing up a strategy, don't try to tackle everything at once. Your findings should enable you to identify the areas most in need of attention. This will help you to put together an incremental programme of improvements.

The McLeod report identified four key enablers of employee engagement:

- leadership
- engaging managers
- voice
- integrity.

The following action points expand on these and outline the areas to consider when developing a strategy for employee engagement.

3 Set a clear vision and strategy

It is easy for leaders to assume that everyone knows and understands what the organisation is for and what it is trying to achieve. But vision and strategy need to be clearly articulated and communicated, so that employees in all areas of the business develop a shared understanding of organisational aims and objectives and understand how their job fits in with and contributes to them. Everyone needs to be able to look beyond the day-to-day work of their own section and get the 'big picture' of what is happening across the organisation.

4 Recognise the role of line managers

For the majority of employees, their most important working relationship is with their line manager. Line managers, therefore, play an important role in engaging employees. Bear in mind that to do this, they must themselves be fully engaged by the senior leadership. They must be able to:

- develop constructive and open working relationships with their team members
- ensure that employees have a clear idea of what is expected of them in their job roles
- facilitate and empower rather than control and restrict
- give feedback on good and poor performance
- express appreciation for the contribution of team members
- provide support, coaching, and opportunities for training and development as necessary.

It is also crucial that line managers are seen to treat employees as individuals, with fairness and respect, and that they show concern for their well-being. Consider whether line managers need training and development in management and leadership skills, especially soft skills, and take account of these characteristics in your recruitment and promotion processes.

5 Make effective communication a priority

Organisations use a range of different methods to keep their employees informed and up-to-date. These include meetings, briefings, newsletters and corporate intranets. What matters in relation to engagement is not so much the methods used, but the effectiveness, regularity and consistency of communication. It should also be open and honest, focusing on positive progress and achievements as well as the challenges and difficulties faced by the organisation. No one likes to feel that they are being kept in the dark or being given a false impression of the true situation. This undermines confidence and trust in leaders and can lead to disillusionment and disengagement.

6 Listen to your employees

Communication should be two-way – being listened to helps employees to understand that they are valued and respected. Employees need to know that their views and opinions will be heard and taken into account, even if not acted upon; that their ideas and suggestions are welcome; and that they can safely raise issues that concern them. It is particularly important for senior managers to be visible and approachable. Some organisations provide email access to senior management so that employees can ask questions or put forward ideas, for example. Others encourage a culture of MBWA (management by walking around).

There are many different ways to consult with employees and develop 'employee voice'. Formal methods include:

- employee suggestion schemes
- staff councils
- workshops and consultations
- partnerships with trade unions.

Whatever methods are used, however, they must be seen as genuine or they will lead to frustration on the part of employees. For example, where a suggestion scheme is introduced, the processes for evaluating suggestions should be clearly defined, suggestions that are accepted should be acted on, and the reasons other suggestions cannot be accepted should be explained.

7 Develop relationships based on trust

Employee engagement is essentially to do with relationships rather than processes and procedures and trust is a vital ingredient, especially in times of uncertainty. It is important for employees to know that their leaders are not just focused on their own personal agendas but have the interests of the whole organisation and its workforce at heart. To earn the trust and loyalty of their employees, leaders and managers must be visible and authentic. They must be seen to speak the truth and act with integrity. If there is a statement of organisational values, leaders should model those values in their own behaviour. As mentioned in point 5, open and honest communication also helps to build trust.

8 Review reward and recognition systems

Studies have shown that financial incentives are not necessarily the prime motivators of commitment and engagement. Nonetheless, perceptions of unfairness can be a powerful disengaging factor. It is important for employees to feel that they are being fairly compensated for their efforts; that pay and reward structures, including bonus schemes, are fair and equitable; and that performance appraisals and performance management systems are applied fairly and consistently across the organisation. Packages of employee benefits can help to create positive attitudes towards an employer, especially where the benefits offered fit the perceived needs of the workforce. Some organisations offer flexible benefits packages which can be tailored to individual needs and priorities.

Recognising the achievements and contributions of employees can also have a significant impact on engagement. This may be informally through expressions of thanks and appreciation, for example on the successful completion of a project, or more formally through schemes involving cash or non-cash rewards such as vouchers or cinema tickets.

9 **Provide learning and development opportunities**

The provision of opportunities for appropriate training and development will help employees develop their skills and work effectively in their current jobs, giving a sense of achievement and job satisfaction. It can also help to identify latent talents and abilities and open up opportunities for promotion and career progression. However, employers should be careful not to give employees false expectations of the career opportunities open to them.

10 **Build a culture of engagement**

Employee engagement is not a one-off exercise. Organisations need to develop and maintain a culture which:

- values and respect its employees
- demonstrates fairness and integrity
- promotes open communication
- encourages participation and involvement.

This will involve regular monitoring of improvements or setbacks and the tackling of issues as they arise.

As a manager you should avoid:

- seeing employee engagement as a 'quick fix' for organisational problems – engagement is a process that requires time, patience and consistency
- regarding employee engagement as a way of manipulating or pressurising employees into working harder – this will ultimately be counter-productive
- seeing a strategy for employee engagement as an add-on or an

optional extra – it needs to be integrated into the culture and daily working practices of the organisation

- thinking that a 'one-size-fits-all' approach is all that is needed
- delegating responsibility for employee engagement to HR or external consultants. While they may have an important contribution to make, employee engagement must be the responsibility of the chief executive and the senior management team at every stage.

Developing trust

Trust can be broadly defined as having confidence in the honesty, integrity and morality of another person, firmly believing that they will act in accordance with what they say. Trust has many aspects, including being trusted to maintain a confidence; having trusted abilities; being trusted to share the same aims; displaying judgement that people can trust; being trusted to give honest feedback; having trustworthy motives and ambitions; and being trusted to deliver what the boss wants on time.

Trust is a fundamental element of any relationship, including that between leaders and their people. Trust is the glue that holds relationships together. When trust is absent, leaders may find that their followers turn to someone else for guidance and direction. Trust is earned and built over time. It can take a long time to establish, yet only moments to destroy – and once lost, trust is extremely difficult to restore.

Trust is two-way: managers need to be able to trust their team to conduct its duties to the highest possible standards and delegate with confidence that the job will be carried out; and followers need to be able to trust their manager to lead them in the right direction to fulfil the objectives of both their department and the wider organisation. They have to be certain that the person leading them is not motivated by a personal agenda but has the best interests of the team and the organisation at the forefront of their decision-making. It is imperative that followers can trust their leaders to defend them when appropriate and can be sure that they are making the right decisions for the right reasons. Establishing a working relationship that is based on trust goes a long way to improving morale, motivation and employee engagement, which in turn leads to increased productivity and performance.

Action checklist

1 Be patient

Trust is not automatically present in a working relationship. It needs to be developed and nurtured over a period of time. The process cannot be rushed, so patience should be exercised until trust has been successfully built. Aim to cultivate trust slowly, ensuring that once you have it you are careful to maintain it. Never take trust for granted. Remember that trust is transient and can be lost more quickly than it is earned.

Developing trust will be particularly difficult if you are taking over a well-established team, especially if your predecessor was a trusted leader. Employees become familiar with the management style and behaviour of a manager, so inevitably the replacement of one leader with another will require a period of adjustment for both parties. In this situation it is crucial to convince your new team that you can be trusted, by showing them that you are in it for the long haul and are committed to delivering on your promises.

2 Demonstrate integrity

Integrity is an essential building block in forming a trusting relationship. You must be honest in your actions and your communications, showing that you are genuine in both. Be honest with yourself and with your team at all times, even when things don't work out as you may have planned. Freely admit when you are wrong or don't know something and reveal your vulnerabilities. This will go a long way to helping you become a trusted leader who is able to be open without fear of reproach.

Never under any circumstances should you lie, even if you feel you have already gained the trust of others. Lying is deceptive. This can have only a negative impact on relationships. Demonstrate your integrity by having the courage to act in accordance with your beliefs and principles, and let others see that you speak from your heart not just your head. The importance of integrity increases with seniority, as others will expect to see you 'live' the values by which both you and the organisation are governed.

3 Communicate openly with your team

Communication is another fundamental element in building trust. Others will find it difficult to trust you if they feel that you are keeping something from them, or that you have some form of hidden agenda. Make your intent clear by communicating in a straightforward way, so that your words are not misunderstood or misinterpreted. Honest and open communication will effectively engage your staff. It is imperative that you are consistent in your communication. Communicating and cascading information will help your team feel that they are included and have the knowledge necessary to fulfil their duties. This will reduce feelings of vulnerability that can arise if they are 'kept in the dark'. If employees feel that the information you are cascading is accurate and timely, they are more likely to trust what you tell them. Communicate with the purpose of sharing knowledge; never deliberately withhold information as a means of control.

4 Get the job done right

For others to trust and believe in you as a leader, it is imperative that you demonstrate you can achieve what you set out to achieve. You may talk a good talk, but until you actually do what you say you will do, your team will find it difficult to believe what you say. If you are consistent in word and deed, you will be well on your way to becoming a trusted leader. It will take time to develop a track record, but aim to start as you mean to go on. By fulfilling the team's expectations of you, you will slowly gain credibility. This will help convince them of your ability to follow through on subsequent ventures and consequently gain their support. Take responsibility for your actions, admitting mistakes when necessary without being defensive, and apologise if necessary. When you can demonstrate that you have the ability to deliver what you promise, you will then begin to build a reputation as a successful leader, who can not only be relied upon to perform but, more importantly, can also be trusted.

5 Consider the bigger picture

To win the trust of others you must show that you have their needs, and those of the organisation, in mind. Don't focus exclusively on your own achievements and objectives. Others will find it difficult to trust a leader who is motivated solely by their own agenda. Let others see that you really care about them and the organisation and you will soon receive their trust and respect. By showing that you are driven by the wider organisational objectives, and those of your immediate team, you will help to develop a culture of trust which will hopefully continue long after your own tenure with the company. Let your team know what targets you have to reach and how this affects the department. They will see the positive impact you are making and understand that you are committed to delivering on your promises.

6 Don't abuse your position

Occupying a position of seniority within an organisation brings with it its own 'granted' power. However, do not use your status as a means of controlling your workforce, as trust cannot be gained in this way. Rather, delegate tasks to others and encourage them to take certain courses of action, as opposed to simply dictating to them. Use your position of power positively to make improvements that will benefit both your team and the wider organisation.

7 Show that you trust your team

The imposition of too many rules and regulations will send the message that you don't really trust your team. You have to demonstrate faith in their professional ability to conduct their duties according to expectations. By demonstrating your trust in them, you make them more likely to respond to your faith in kind. Don't undermine your position as a trusted leader by needless employee monitoring. Instead, trust your team to take authority for their areas of responsibility and to make decisions commensurate with their role. Refrain from interfering with the work of others, unless you feel that their actions are detrimental. Aim to create an environment where trust is reciprocated so that you can effectively engage your staff and boost productivity.

8 Encourage the sharing of ideas

Your team need to be able to trust you before they will share their thoughts. You are responsible for the welfare of your staff and thus it is vital that they can trust you. Show your staff that you are genuinely interested in them, their opinions and their welfare and that you can be trusted to keep a confidence. Never betray a confidence or engage in tittle-tattle about others. Provide the opportunity for your staff to express their views and listen with genuine interest. Be open to the perspectives of others without being judgemental. Aim to create an atmosphere where people feel comfortable sharing their thoughts and ideas without fear of recrimination, even if they express opinions that are at odds with yours. Trust others to communicate and they will reciprocate by trusting you. You must also develop sound listening skills. Listening to the views and ideas of others will develop a trusting relationship, especially if you act upon their feelings and show that you are giving them just consideration.

9 Deal with poor performance

You must address poor performance in order to be credible to others. Be consistent in your approach to discipline, ensuring that you are fair at all times. Eliminate feelings of discrimination or favouritism. Trust and respect go hand in hand. Do all you can to ensure that this happens. Try not to develop a culture of blame. Challenge your team when necessary without being antagonistic, and aim to gain an understanding of their actions and their perspective, rather than blaming them.

10 Be consistent

Be consistent in your communication, actions, attitudes and behaviour. This will enable others to anticipate how you will react and respond in a given situation and reassure them that you will not act unpredictably. If you behave inconsistently, they will be unable to easily anticipate your reaction. This will make them suspicious and wary, and will develop a culture of uncertainty rather than one of trust.

As a manager you should avoid:

- 'talking the talk' without following through on promises
- betraying a confidence
- using authority as a means of control
- being inconsistent
- ignoring poor performance
- taking trust for granted
- forgetting that trust is fragile and can be destroyed more quickly than it can be earned.

Undertaking employee attitude surveys

An employee attitude survey is a planned procedure that enables managers to explore employees' opinions on particular issues and on the organisation, so as to be able to take account of them in the planning process, or to make changes that will be beneficial to both the organisation and the individuals who work within it.

Employee attitude surveys are used by organisations to monitor employees' views, or gauge the effects of a new policy, such as implementing a performance-related pay scheme. Such surveys can be carried out on a routine, regular basis, or as a one-off, for occasional purposes. Employees should not, however, be surveyed too often; eighteen months is generally agreed as a good minimum period between surveys.

You need plenty of time and resources to plan, carry out and evaluate an employee attitude survey. Reassure employees that there is no 'hidden agenda' involved, and let them know your reasons for doing a survey. Employee attitude surveys have many uses, such as:

- providing data for problem solving, planning and decision-making
- engaging employees and improving morale and motivation
- increasing managers' awareness of people's opinions and feelings
- providing an effective communication medium or sounding-board.

It is vital that the results of an employee attitude survey are reported back to employees, and that the organisation is seen to act on them.

Action checklist

1 Define the scope and coverage of the survey

Identify the subject on which employees' opinions are to be gathered. Be as precise as possible and be clear on how you will deal with people's views once they have been given. Bear in mind that a survey entitled, for example, 'Introducing Teleworking', may give rise to all sorts of anxieties or expectations.

Decide who is to be included in the survey: all employees, one department, a single site, or a group of employees.

2 Decide who is to run the survey

The survey could be run by your personnel or HR department, if you have one that is large enough, or by a special working party drawn from all levels in the organisation. You could also consider contracting out the work to an external consultant, if you feel you lack the necessary expertise internally; this will cost more, but it may help to convince employees of the impartiality of the process and that the results will be acted upon.

3 Select a survey method

Two principal survey methods are available:

- questionnaires, to be filled in by individual employees – these are particularly useful when there are large numbers of employees to survey and the required information is of a 'yes/no' type

- interviews with employees – these can be carried out with either individuals or groups, and the interactive contact involved allows for a deeper exploration of attitudes. The process is time-consuming, however, and can be impractical with large numbers. It is also likely to produce inconsistencies, and its final results will be harder to quantify.

Consider the numbers to be surveyed, the type of information needed and the resources available. If you aim to use computer software for analysing results, find out more about what is available before designing your questionnaire or deciding on your interview approach.

4 Determine the questions and procedures

Your questionnaire or interview guidelines should be formulated carefully, with clarity and lack of ambiguity in mind. Further points to consider include:

- How long will it take for employees to complete?
- Do the questions cover the subject adequately?
- Do any questions discriminate against any group of employees?
- Will the information obtained be easy to analyse?
- Is confidentiality assured?
- Do you want to standardise some questions, so that useful trend data can be gathered year-on-year?
- Will it be helpful to ask if individuals would be prepared to answer follow-up questions for further exploration? If so, you will need to provide the opportunity for them to identify themselves at the end of the survey.

Take account of any possible problems with literacy or understanding of terminology, and remember that seemingly simple questions can hold many pitfalls for those new to devising questionnaires or survey interviews. Find out more about the process, or take professional advice, before finalising questions and procedures.

5 Pilot the survey

Piloting the survey is a must, to check how respondents interpret the questions. Select a number of employees and ask them to complete a questionnaire or undertake an interview. Find out if they prefer to think about it at work or take it home, and afterwards ask them if they had any problems in completing the survey. See whether the information obtained is what was being looked for. If necessary, make modifications to the questionnaire, or provide extra training for the interviewers.

6 Explain the exercise to all employees

It is crucial to ensure that people understand your reasons for carrying out the survey and appreciate the benefits it may have. This will alleviate possible fears and should result in a higher response rate. Depending on the nature of the survey, you may also wish to explain why you are doing it to those not participating.

7 Implement the survey

Distribute the questionnaires or arrange the interviews and, to avoid loss of impetus, leave as short a time as feasible for the survey to be completed. Remember, though, to allow sufficient time for its completion by any employees on leave, and to ensure that help is on hand to deal with possible problems. You could ask people to return completed questionnaires to an outside agency to persuade them that their replies will be dealt with in confidence and with impartiality.

8 Collate and report results

It is essential to communicate the results of the survey to both senior managers and employees, if distrust and suspicion are to be avoided. For employees, it is usually advisable to provide only a summary, as most will not wish to read a lengthy document. Ensure employees are told of promised plans of action resulting from the survey. If possible, benchmark the results externally, especially for regular surveys that monitor trends. If the survey is quite specific, however, comparisons may be impossible. Analytical software can be used for all types of surveys, but if you have little knowledge of social research methods, you could contract out the analysis.

9 Evaluate the survey method

Evaluate the survey after completion, covering, for example, the response rate and any difficulties that arose. Take account of the findings when planning and designing a follow-up or a new employee attitude survey.

10 Follow-up survey method

It is often desirable to undertake a second, follow-up survey once the plans of action following the first have had time to take effect. This can help with evaluating whether or not changes introduced as a result of the survey have led to improvements. (In cases where little action is called for this stage is unnecessary.)

As a manager you should avoid:

- implementing an employee attitude survey without careful planning or initial piloting
- forgetting to note problems encountered, for future reference
- failing to report results of the survey and plans of action to all employees.

Robert R. Blake and Jane S. Mouton

The Managerial Grid©

Introduction

Robert R. Blake and Jane Srygley Mouton worked together at the psychology department of the University of Texas during the 1950s and 1960s. They are known primarily for the development of the managerial grid as a framework for understanding managerial behaviour. They subsequently set up a company, Scientific Methods Inc., to disseminate their ideas on organisational development and management effectiveness.

Lives and careers

Blake was born in 1918 and studied psychology at Berea College, University of Virginia, where he took his MA in 1941, then at the University of Texas at Austin, where he took his PhD in 1947. He stayed at the University of Texas as a professor until 1964, receiving an LLD in 1992.

Mouton studied pure mathematics and physics at the University of Texas and received an MA in psychology from Florida State University in 1951 and a PhD from the University of Texas in 1957. Blake and Mouton developed the concept of the managerial grid while working together at the University of Texas, and their ideas were tested and developed through the implementation of an organisational development programme at Exxon, an American oil corporation.

In 1955, Blake and Mouton founded Scientific Methods to provide consultancy services based on the workplace application of ideas from behavioural science. The company was formally incorporated in 1961, and grew to offer grid-based organisation development and consultancy programmes in the areas of individual learning, team development, conflict resolution and strategic modelling in over thirty countries worldwide.

Blake and Mouton's collaboration continued until Mouton's death in 1987. They published numerous articles and about forty books describing their theories and applying them in a variety of contexts. Blake also lectured at Harvard, Oxford and Cambridge, and worked on special projects as a Fulbright Scholar at the Tavistock Clinic in London. In 1997, Blake and the estate of Jane Mouton sold Scientific Methods to a long-time grid associate. The company was renamed Grid International Inc. and still promotes grid organisation development around the world. Blake remained involved with the company as an associate until his death in 2004.

The Managerial Grid

Blake and Mouton set out to apply the ideas of behavioural scientists such as Rensis Likert to the practice of management. They built on studies conducted at Ohio State University and the University of Michigan in the 1940s which attempted to identify the behavioural characteristics of successful leaders. Blake and Mouton identified two fundamental drivers of managerial behaviour: concern for getting the job done, and concern for the people doing the work. They argued that, on the one hand, an exclusive concern for production at the expense of the needs of those engaged in production leads to dissatisfaction and conflict, thus adversely affecting performance; but that, on the other hand, an excessive concern to avoid conflict and maintain good relationships is also detrimental to the achievement of goals and objectives.

To provide a framework for describing management behaviours,

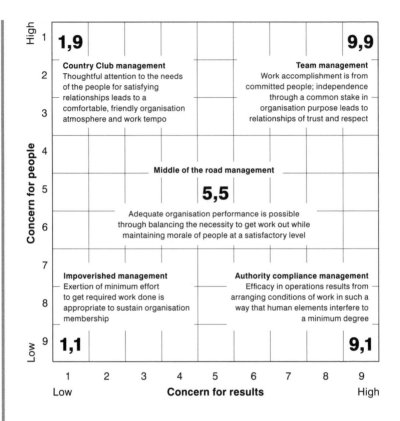

Figure 1: The leadership grid

the two variables of 'concern for production' and 'concern for people' were plotted on a grid showing nine degrees of concern for each, from 1, indicating a low level of concern, to 9, indicating a high level of concern. Five positions on the grid represent five differing managerial behaviour patterns (see figure).

The bottom right corner of the grid represents a 9,1 style of management: maximum concern for the efficient accomplishment of tasks, but minimum concern for human relationships. This pattern corresponds to the traditional authority-based style of command and control management. The 1,9 position at the top left, in contrast, focuses on human relations at the cost of efficient production, and has been called the 'country club' style of management; 1,1 management – minimum concern for either production or people – is characterised by a desire to avoid responsibility and exert minimum effort. The 5,5 manager attempts to maintain a balance between both concerns, but 9,9 management, which integrates maximum attention to both people and production, is put forward as the most effective approach.

As a further refinement to grid theory, additional managerial styles combining two or more of the basic styles are identified. For example, paternalism is defined as 9,1–1,9 management where the manager swings between two extremes. There is a need to control and dominate and resistance is met with reprimand. At the other extreme, compliance is reinforced by recognition and appreciation.

Grid organisation development programmes

While the managerial grid was considered useful in helping managers to understand their own behaviour patterns, it was recognised that only so much could be achieved through individual management development, and that problems needed to be addressed at work group and organisational level. Consequently, grid theory was used as a starting point for the development of organisation development programmes designed to enhance managerial effectiveness, resolve conflict and develop teamwork within the organisation.

The programmes follow a six-phase approach:

1 Grid seminar
2 Team development

3 Inter-group development

4 Goal setting and strategy development

5 Implementation

6 Stabilisation

The grid seminar generates awareness of how personal behaviours have an impact on others in the workplace. Participants learn and practise specific skills in teams, and engage in a structured critique that measures activity results on several levels. The skills are common-sense ones in any workplace, and include, for example, the best ways to take initiative, resolve conflict, or make sound decisions. Participants use grid theory to clarify personal values and attitudes regarding behaviours, and then work in teams to complete structured activities under time and performance pressures. The seminar is over 90% experiential, placing the responsibility for learning, practice and change in the hands of participants. This level of team involvement and responsibility is found to make the learning effective and lasting.

Phases two and three focus on problem solving and conflict resolution, both within and between work groups. A major concern is to enable teams to develop the ability to work together towards a common goal in a synergistic way. In phase four the focus moves to reaching agreement on broader, organisation-wide goals. Planned changes are implemented in phase five, and in the final phase progress is monitored to ensure that the changes continue in the workplace and are consolidated and stabilised. This programme is applied throughout the organisation at all levels, and in large organisations the process may take three to five years to complete. In the course of the programme, the focus moves from the behaviour of individual managers to the effectiveness of work groups and teams, and the involvement of the whole organisation.

Over the years the concepts and principles of grid organisation development were refined and applied in a variety of fields.

Several new editions of *The Managerial Grid* were published, as well as books covering the use of grid programmes in areas such as sales management, academic administration, real estate, social work, medicine and even marriage. More recent publications emphasised the application of grid principles to areas of topical interest, such as teambuilding, change and stress management.

Synergogy

Blake and Mouton also developed their own educational theories on how best to teach grid theories and concepts in the work group context. These are described in their book *Synergogy*, published in 1984. The term 'synergogy', coined by Blake and Mouton, describes a systematic approach to learning that leads team members to learn from each other in a cooperative and participative way. Synergogy, defined as 'working together for shared teaching', was contrasted to pedagogy, where instruction is given by a teacher, and andragogy, where the teacher acts as a facilitator.

Four synergogic learning designs were developed to provide a structure for the process of learning. The 'Team Effectiveness Design' and the 'Team Member Teaching Design' relate to the acquisition of knowledge. The 'Performance Judging Design' relates to the development of skills. Lastly, the 'Clarifying Attitudes Design' concerns awareness and development of appropriate attitudes. Techniques employed include individual preparation, presentations, multiple choice and true/false tests and team discussion. The role of the learning administrator is limited to making sure that the learning design is effectively implemented. These methods were first used by Blake and Mouton to teach university courses but were later adapted to workplace training sessions.

In perspective

The management grid is regarded as one of the first attempts to define appropriate management behaviours. Blake and Mouton's approach to organisation development focuses on human behavioural processes rather than technological and structural aspects of organisations. There is an underlying supposition that a single, universally applicable leadership style will fit all situations.

The theoretical basis of Blake and Mouton's approach has sometimes been questioned, and critics have pointed to a lack of substantial research evidence for the effectiveness of grid organisation development programmes. Testimonial evidence, however, is not lacking and grid programmes continue to have widespread appeal. Over 2 million copies of grid publications have been sold, and grid programmes have been implemented in world-class companies, such as BP and ICI. The grid concept has helped managers grasp the ideas being presented, and the direct practical approach embodied in grid development programmes has made them more accessible than theoretical approaches.

Blake and Mouton's ideas focus on the behaviour of individual managers and have been presented as embodying common-sense wisdom. This has undoubtedly helped them to gain acceptance, and their influence has been substantial in Europe, Asia and North America. Their success, however, is often seen to be due more to their marketing expertise than to the originality of their ideas.

The development and promotion of the grid seminar represents a key stage in the history of promoting management ideas, and is a prime example of the role of packaging and branding. Scientific Methods successfully segmented the market for organisation development with the application of the grid principles in a variety of sectors.

Managing creativity

The terms creativity and innovation are often used interchangeably. However, making a clear distinction between the two helps to understand them clearly so that they can be better managed.

Creativity has been described as the formation and gathering of thoughts in a way that leads to a different understanding of a situation. Innovation is more often associated with the development of a new product or service. The concepts are distinct but they fit together: creativity is the process of generating new ideas; while innovation relates more to the process of implementing new ideas for the benefit of the organisation.

An organisation's ability to innovate by developing and exploiting people's creativity and generating new ideas is generally considered a key to competitive advantage, particularly in the context of rapid change in business and society. It is essential, therefore, for organisations to continually foster and manage creativity and innovation if they are to achieve and sustain success in the marketplace.

Creativity has not always occupied a significant place in management theory and practice, and it used to be the case that a lack of control was seen as a threat to organisational well-being. Now, however, a lack of flexibility and too much control are perceived as dangers, and the exercise of personal creativity is encouraged along with the careful management of creativity to unlock its optimum value.

This checklist focuses on organisational processes, steps and techniques for managing creativity in others, rather than on developing one's own creativity.

Consider these examples:

● Manager A is a highly creative individual who assails his/her team with ideas to the point where they cannot keep up with the flow.

● Manager B has few creative ideas but is highly effective at listening, encouraging and helping people to come up with ideas that can then be put to the test.

This checklist is concerned mainly to support and develop manager B and to provide guidance on managing creativity in an organisational context.

Action checklist

1 Identify potential sources of ideas, or stimuli to creativity

● **Research** has tended to be associated more with the invention of products, but it is just as likely to come up with ideas for new processes as well as products. This could be academic research papers, newspaper reports, or the latest article from a trade or professional journal.

● **Employees** handle the day-to-day problems, processes and plaudits; they are the key to spotting opportunities or threats, better ways of doing things, or ways of doing different things.

● **Customers** may not always be right, but it is vital to stay close, listen and explore their comments, feedback and complaints. In recent years, online networking technologies have opened up new ways to connect with users of your products and services and take advantage of their ideas and suggestions.

● **Relationships** with suppliers can develop into partnerships, which can be used for mutual benefit.

● **Competitors** will have their own agenda for creativity; actively seeking out intelligence on a competitor's activities can provide an early alert to new developments.

● **Happenstance** – it has been said that creativity probably stems more from a situation that is unplanned and undirected, be it in the bath or on the golf course. Whatever the source, an idea is an idea, until putting it to the test demonstrates that it won't work.

2 Set an example

This is a matter of attitude and approach rather than being creative yourself, although that can obviously help now and again. Set an example by:

● encouraging new ideas consistently rather than when, or if, you have the time

● discussing all ideas in open forum, not just those that you think are good

● welcoming new explorations and different directions rather than enforcing a policy of unchanging stability

● looking out for new ways of working rather than always relying on the tried and tested.

Although you may be the team leader, become a team member as well. Challenge others about the way they do things, even about what they are doing, and encourage them to challenge you. You need to adopt a number of different roles to get the best from teams. You may find it useful to alternate between:

● the manager who sits back, listens and encourages, and knows when to move away from an unprofitable track

● the communicator who interprets input from different individuals

● the devil's advocate who is trying to get people to see that there is an alternative

● the builder who makes links between a number of options

● the coordinator who sums up when a consensus begins to appear.

3 Be aware of team members' personalities and cognitive styles

Some team members may appear more openly creative; others may express their creativity in more subtle ways, or need active encouragement. Adaptation–innovation theory, developed by Michael J. Kirton, suggests that all people solve problems and are creative, but that they do this in different ways: adaptors prefer a more structured approach; innovators are more likely to think 'outside the box'. An awareness and acceptance of such differences can help teams to function creatively.

4 Develop a climate for creativity

Creativity thrives best in an environment of openness and interaction. While this is difficult to put into words, it has to do with:

- a sense of dynamism, hustle and bustle rather than a hush in the air

- an atmosphere of mutual respect and trust where people feel free to interact, rather than a climate of deference to rank or position

- not allowing rules and procedures to control activities rigidly and inflexibly

- a sense of individual energy, enthusiasm, open-mindedness and commitment, which uses conflicting ideas constructively (while minimising personal conflict).

5 Use techniques for creativity

A number of techniques which may be used to develop creativity and generate ideas are listed below. All have their strengths and weaknesses and there are conflicting views of their benefits. It is important to evaluate any techniques you plan to use and choose those that you feel will work well in your context.

- **Lateral thinking.** Pioneered by Edward de Bono, this takes us outside our familiar, organisational way of reasoning and opens up many different ways of thinking about a problem.

This approach requires logic and analysis, but challenges and tests the assumptions that tend to govern our 'normal' thought processes.

- **Mind-mapping.** Pioneered by Tony Buzan, this mirrors the way in which the brain stores and retrieves information. It is a powerful means of expressing the thought patterns, pictures and associations that exist in the brain.

- **Brainstorming.** Invented by Alex Osborn, this involves spontaneous, open-ended discussion in the search for new ideas. It is widely used and can generate large numbers of ideas, but it has been criticised for attempting to produce ideas too quickly, leading to dull and poor-quality results.

- **Rich pictures.** Developed by Peter Checkland as the starting point for soft systems methodology, this provides a means of capturing and expressing unstructured and 'messy' situations.

- **Focus groups.** These can be used to explore a particular topic in greater depth, allowing people to develop related ideas as they go along and build on the views expressed by others. Participants can be encouraged to think laterally rather than sticking to the usual line of thought.

6 Build in breathing time/space

There is no secret here: if you want people to be creative, you can't expect to see them 'doing' all the time. People need 'white space' for thinking and time to explore different approaches in different ways. Creativity is more likely to thrive when there is time for reflection than in a stressed and pressurised working environment. If you trust people with space and time, generally they will be more able to come up with new ideas and fresh approaches.

7 Build systems for creativity

Organisational systems can smother or hinder creativity, especially if their structures are cumbersome and bureaucratic. However, it is also possible to identify processes and systems that will facilitate creativity and build them into your working practices. These may include the following:

- **360 degree appraisal.** Constructive reviews are conducted on a regular, honest and open basis and feedback from customers, subordinates, peers and managers is discussed.

- **Self-directed teams.** Small groups of people are genuinely empowered to manage themselves and the work they do. Such groups require flexibility and support from the organisation, and multi-skills and self-discipline from the team members.

- **Flexible working.** Standard working hours may no longer be appropriate in all cases. Introducing greater flexibility as to when, where and how work is carried out and gearing work to the employee rather than vice versa can improve morale and release creative energy.

8 Work out inexpensive pilots

It is important to try out ideas that seem to promise much but may need significant investment. Find ways to pilot such ideas on a small scale so that you can put them to the test, gain evidence to justify the investment required and draw lessons from the initial phase, which will be of benefit to later, fuller implementations. Departmental applications, telephone surveys of existing customers and seed corn money can all be used to lay a foundation for innovation while avoiding unnecessary expenditure.

9 Feedback and reward

Feedback and reward can play a crucial role in encouraging creativity and innovation. Let employees know how their suggestions are turning out and keep them informed on progress. Feedback should be constructive and encouraging, and cover all the ideas that employees have contributed.

The creative process is often complex and can be seen as chaotic and unmanageable. It is all too easy for creativity to be stifled unintentionally by a pervasive resistance to change or an inflexible approach.

As a manager you should avoid:

- assuming that all the best ideas come from the top
- dismissing ideas out of hand without evaluating them
- ignoring suggestions for small changes – they may nonetheless lead to major improvements
- forgetting to give feedback on ideas whatever the outcome
- failing to involve employees in the implementation of ideas
- excessive rigidity in the application of rules and regulations
- reluctance to move beyond formal job descriptions
- a culture of blame where failure is penalised rather than being seen as an opportunity to learn
- overreliance on financial incentives and rewards – creative people enjoy a challenge and tend to be motivated by intrinsic rewards.

Redundancy: managing the survivors

'Survivors' in the context of redundancy are those employees who remain with an organisation after it has gone through a restructuring or redundancy programme.

Restructuring or redundancy programmes are now all too common. Redundancies will always be a shock for employees, including those whose own jobs are not being made redundant. While it is essential to ensure that redundancies are handled fairly and that employees are consulted where this is appropriate and/or required by law, it is also critical to consider the interests of those who are staying with the organisation and to communicate a positive vision for the future.

To some extent, redundancies are bound to have a negative effect on morale, but this can be much reduced by well-communicated and carefully thought-out management policies. These have the power to reduce the detrimental effects on corporate and individual morale and performance, and increase the likelihood that key employees will stay with the organisation. Communicating changes openly, and letting people understand that their interests have been taken into consideration where possible, will enable you to reduce the negative impacts for all.

The direct cost of a careless approach to redundancies is high, but indirect costs may be even higher. Lowered morale, higher absenteeism and general demotivation can lead to corresponding poor organisational performance and productivity. This checklist offers guidance on how managers can support, encourage, motivate and retain remaining employees or survivors, following a restructuring or redundancy programme.

Action checklist

1 Understand the pattern of responses to loss or change

Various models of emotional responses to change or loss suggest that we all go through similar patterns of emotions and reactions (see figure).

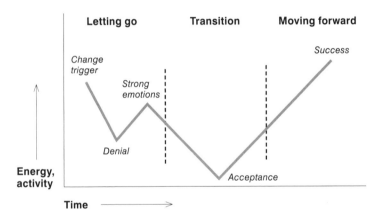

Figure 2: Typical emotional response patterns following major change

Responses may differ from one person to the next and the stages may overlap, vary in order and/or be missed out altogether, but a common pattern seems to be:

- initial disbelief and denial, followed by strong and varied emotions
- apathy, depression and despair, as the situation is accepted
- acceptance of, and adaptation to, a changed reality.

Working through these emotions seems to be vital for helping people to move on and take a positive approach to the future.

2 Consider what survivors are feeling

Though their own jobs are not redundant, survivors are affected by the changes they witness. They may also experience direct effects such as additional work arising from the redundancies. Remember that progression through the various emotions is rarely smooth, and people can be unsettled for months after a change. Their feelings may include:

- relief that they are still employed
- guilt that they are employed while colleagues are out of work
- fear of future redundancies that might affect them
- exhaustion linked to additional work and uncertain circumstances
- confusion or uncertainty, if rumours take the place of honest communication
- stress if they are left to pick up the pieces without support
- resentment if their contribution is unnoticed
- anxiety about future career developments.

3 Consider survivor needs and communicate, communicate

You need to ensure that survivors have:

- time and attention – be available to listen, even if you can't resolve the problems
- clear direction – ensure that people you manage are clear about their jobs and goals, and understand your expectations
- reasonable workloads – look at ways of streamlining work so it can be handled more effectively
- the latest news and information – let people know what is happening, giving as much information as often as you can
- commitment – show the organisation is concerned about their future, perhaps through a personal and career development focus
- enjoyable work – constant gloom and doom is depressing; people work best when they enjoy it.

4 Avoid stress or overwork

Keep track of people's hours and watch for signs of stress. Encourage employees to take time to relax, and suggest medical help if necessary. Feeling stressed is normal if work pressures are too high, so no one should feel ashamed about needing help with this. But, ideally, resolve the overwork issues quickly.

5 Seek savings of time or effort

Review processes to eliminate duplication or blockages. Look out for:

● handovers between your area and other functions – the more there are, the more the possibility of delay or error

● similar activities carried out by different functions or departments – trade-offs could achieve more efficiency

● logging and record-keeping – check that records are necessary, brief and do not duplicate each other

● automation possibilities – consider whether it is feasible and worthwhile to automate time-consuming manual processes.

Ask those doing the work for ideas on how to improve processes and consider time management courses if people think it might help them.

6 Create a positive vision for the future

Employees may be uncertain about how changes will affect them, what will be expected of them and what plans there are for the future of their section or department and the wider organisation. This can lead to confusion and insecurity, so make sure that these issues are clearly addressed. Without being unrealistic, look too for any positive aspects of the situation and help employees focus on these. Set short-term and longer-term objectives that people can focus on and work towards.

7 Develop your employees

Helping people to learn and develop is a good way to retain and motivate them. Work-based development activities include coaching, new tasks or activities, work shadowing and cross-functional projects. Investment in qualifications or courses would demonstrate your faith in individuals and in the organisation's future.

8 Recognise and reward achievements

Recognise efforts and achievements to motivate people more. Money is one form of recognition, but genuine praise and appreciation for a job well done are also effective and will build up your relationships with team members. Remember that people often leave a job because their manager fails to recognise them or reward their achievements appropriately. If you need people to stay for a specific period (to complete a project, for example), consider using retention bonuses to tie them in for the time required.

9 Keep communicating

Maintaining communication and contact is not a one-off activity. Continue to make yourself available for those who need to speak to you privately, and hold regular team and one-to-one meetings:

- to review progress and explore potential problems
- to focus on work and 'gel' as a team.

Examples of issues to cover at meetings include passing on corporate news and information and seeking ideas for improvements. You might also wish to arrange informal training sessions. Keep the meetings focused, with strict time limits, such as half-an-hour or an hour a week.

Working alongside your team, where possible, could also improve communication and motivation. Experiencing workload peaks will make you more a part of the team, and give you more understanding of the pressures and challenges they face.

10 Consider your own needs

The points above apply to you as well as your team – redundancy programmes are stressful for managers, too. Relieve pressures by discussing your feelings with someone you trust (taking care to maintain confidentiality), and ask for additional information, support or recognition from your manager, if you need to.

As a manager you should avoid:

- leaving survivors to cope on their own
- forgetting about your own needs – managers are also employees
- trying to take everything upon yourself.

Work–life balance

Work–life balance is the equilibrium between the amount of time and effort a person devotes to work and that given to other aspects of life.

The need for employees to have a reasonable balance between work and other aspects of life is now widely accepted. Work–life balance is seen to have real business benefits, including increased productivity, improvements in performance and competitiveness, better morale, and a lower incidence of stress, absenteeism and sickness. It can help to enhance employee motivation and retention and support recruitment. In the UK, it is now government policy to promote work–life balance and in particular to support working families.

Work–life balance – in particular flexible working practices and family-friendly policies – has been the subject of widespread public debate. This has come about as a result of social and economic changes, such as greater numbers of women in the workforce, the expectations of Generation X (born between the early 1960s and early 1980s) and Generation Y (born between the early 1980s and the early 2000s) employees, the rise of the 24/7 society and technological advances. There has also been a growing backlash against what has been called a 'long-hours culture', which puts employees under pressure to work additional hours, regardless of the impact on their personal lives, health or well-being.

For employers it is important to consider how to give employees more control over their working arrangements, to accommodate other aspects of their lives, without adversely affecting the capability of the organisation to deliver on targets and objectives. It is important, when introducing work–life balance policies, to balance the benefits to individual employees with arrangements to manage the operational implications. This checklist takes an organisational approach to work–life balance, covering assessment of the needs of employees and the establishment of work–life policies and benefit arrangements.

Action checklist

1 Find out what employees' needs are and how far they are being met

Find out what types of work/home conflicts your employees are experiencing. You might assess, for example, personal circumstances, such as the proportion of employees with young children or elderly dependants, and the impact of home commitments in terms of time absent from work. Exit interviews can be used to find out whether work–life balance issues are contributing to the departure of employees. You could also set up focus groups or conduct surveys, explaining why you are doing so, and follow up with the results. Use the results to establish a business case for improving work–life balance which can be related to the bottom line. Communicate your intentions to the most influential people in the organisation and to interested parties such as staff associations and trade unions. Involving employees from the start will help overcome resistance to change, as will ensuring that your work–life policy is inclusive and that every individual can benefit from it.

Before proceeding, it is important to identify the financial resources and personnel needed to implement the policy and maintain it. At the same time, consider the implications of not offering flexible arrangements, such as the loss of key employees and the costs of recruitment and training.

2 Focus on organisation culture

The culture and atmosphere of your organisation need to be conducive to flexibility, innovative work practices and empowerment. Focus on building values. Remember that people work not just for money but also because they get satisfaction from doing the right things. Give them a reason to do what they are doing. Managers need to ensure that flexible benefits are not abused, but employees must not be made to feel disloyal, or that they will be regarded as poor performers, if they take advantage of the benefits. The emphasis should be on outputs and outcomes – that is, performance and results – rather than inputs and presenteeism.

Look at the organisation structure, and consider whether it enables or constrains work–life balance. A traditional hierarchy with a command-and-control approach may not be suited to effective implementation of the new measures that may be necessary. A flatter organisation, in which employees work in teams and are empowered, may make this easier.

It is important for managers to set a good example, and for work–life balance to be integrated into the culture of the organisation at all levels, not just the lower grades.

3 Improve personal and organisational efficiency

An important part of achieving work–life balance is ensuring that the work part of the equation is carried out as smoothly as possible. Time management, delegation, prioritising, and handling information to avoid overload are all skills that can reduce both the stress experienced and the hours worked, while maintaining the same level of productivity. This could have a positive effect on home life, for example by eliminating the need to take work home.

Consider ways in which organisational procedures and activities could be improved to make employees' working lives less frenetic, stressful and tiring.

Consider the possibility that in flatter, less hierarchical

organisations, flexible working arrangements may result in some employees taking on more so that others can do less.

4　Set up work–life policies and benefit arrangements

There is no one approach that will create balance: a flexible set of policies should be set up to cover as many aspects and different situations as possible. Consider the following:

- **Flexible working hours.** Allow employees to organise their working hours to accommodate important aspects of their home lives.

- **Self-rostering.** Allow teams of employees to negotiate and agree their own hours to accommodate each other's needs. Compromises may be needed here.

- **Buddy system.** Pair people up so that they can cover for each other. This enables each to take time off when necessary, knowing that someone else will take over their duties and responsibilities.

- **Flexible working location.** Remote working brings its own set of challenges for organisations and individuals. However, working from a different office or from home, either permanently or on an ad hoc basis, may help employees cope with family responsibilities and reduce or eliminate commuting time.

- **Special leave availability.** Consider, for example, an allowance of paid or unpaid leave each year to give employees time to cope with personal crises or family and household emergencies without using up their holiday allowance.

- **Career breaks.** These can be of varying length, and may be used for study, travel, bringing up children, voluntary work or other activities that improve both home and working life.

- **Health, well-being and employee assistance programmes.** Offer counselling and advice services, not just for work-related issues. Private health insurance and gym subsidies could also be considered.

- **Childcare/eldercare subsidies.** A workplace nursery may not be feasible, but subsidised places in local nurseries or nursing homes may be an option.

It may not be possible to cater for every situation, but in this case a flexible benefits package could be considered. One way to do this is to make a list of priced benefits and give each employee a fixed annual allowance to 'buy' whichever ones they choose. Alternatively, certain benefits could be bought from salary as required.

Take employees' ideas into account. If an employee can make a business case for a change to their way of working, the idea should be tested. This kind of suggestion scheme may prove more responsive to individual circumstances than a rigid set of policies, particularly if tied to monetary reward. This can be of real benefit to business profitability.

5 Inform and train managers

Success depends not just on the policies chosen but also on how they are implemented. This must be consistent across the organisation. Managers should receive training in the range of benefits available and in providing guidance to employees on combinations that will work well. Work–life issues could be incorporated into annual training plans and performance appraisals. Bear in mind that balance cannot be imposed, but that managers can assist employees in deciding on the most appropriate options. It should be stressed that take-up of flexible benefits will not affect promotion prospects, recognition, or other job opportunities.

6 Communicate the policies and benefits

Inform employees of the options available. Consider posting details on the company intranet.

7 Evaluate work–life balance success by measuring employee and customer satisfaction

It is important to maintain the advantages of a good work–life policy by keeping it relevant and up-to-date. You can evaluate its effectiveness by measuring employee satisfaction and performance and assessing factors such as retention rate. The policy should have a positive impact on the company's bottom line, on staff and customer satisfaction and retention, and on the climate within the organisation.

Do not limit performance evaluation to an annual review. Consider meeting every four months to check how things are going. Careful monitoring, feedback and adjustment will ensure the policies work well.

As a manager you should avoid:

- trying to impose work–life balance, or introduce it without consultation and cooperation
- assuming that work–life balance is relevant only to women with children or employees with elderly dependants
- thinking that flexibility is only appropriate to certain work settings
- wrapping up the new arrangements in bureaucratic procedures – accessing the new arrangements should be simple and straightforward.

An introduction to implementing flexible working hours

'Flexibility' covers any variation in working hours other than the standard 9–5 working day. The main variants include: flexible working hours; term-time working; annual hours; job sharing; voluntary reduced work time; employment breaks; and sabbaticals.

Flexible working hours can allow people and time to be managed more effectively, and may help organisations meet peaks and troughs in demand or new customer requirements. Flexibility can be useful for recruiting and retaining the best employees, and staff retention will, in turn, help businesses gain higher returns on training investment. Flexible working hours will support increased workforce diversity and equality of opportunities – for example, disabled people, or those with caring duties, will find it easier to work on a flexible basis.

Punctuality problems and absenteeism should be reduced, once staff can use flexitime to deal with personal appointments or minor crises. Also, a well-managed, flexible working system can increase people's sense of responsibility, leading to better time management, more efficiency during core hours and reduced overtime.

This checklist provides an introduction to some flexible working practices and explains how to organise their implementation.

There are various different types of flexible working, some covering special cases or needs and others involving 'normal' working hours that can be carried forward or back to allow extra time off. Well-known examples of the major types are given below, together with their main advantages:

- **Term-time working** facilitates availability to work, usually for people with younger children.

- **Employment breaks** help retain the service of people who need a temporary break from work.

- **Sabbaticals** enable employees to fulfil study or travel ambitions and then return to work.

- **Voluntary reduced work time** opens up flexible work to a wider range of people.

- **Compressed hours** allows the hours worked to be completed within a shorter time period – for example, a four-day week or a nine-day fortnight.

- **Annual hours** reduces the overall number of hours and overtime worked and may increase productivity by making seasonal variations easier to manage.

- **Job sharing** gives employers more continuity in cases of sickness or leave – and job sharers can be fresher and more enthusiastic than full-time employees.

Action checklist

1 Secure the commitment of senior management

Ensure that senior managers are aware of the rationale for introducing flexibility and the business case for it. Reach agreement with them on the extent of flexibility and ensure they are committed to this.

2 Draw up a profile of the existing workforce and their current hours

Unless you profile the hours worked by your existing workforce, you may not realise the extent to which line managers already sanction informal flexible working time.

3 Decide how flexible the organisation can afford to be

Decide whether you are considering all options for flexibility or want to limit employees to a fixed range. Flexitime, for example, should apply to everyone at all levels, but core, non-flexible hours can be specified if you wish. Once flexible working options are adopted, it is hard to withdraw them, so pilot the scheme and expand it gradually.

4 Consult all employees

Once you know what sort of flexible working pattern(s) would fit best in your business, present your ideas to employees to determine whether the system would be acceptable to them. You might use questionnaires, workshops or discussion groups to test employees' views and gain their feedback.

5 Consider a working group to represent all levels and types of employee

If the implementation of a flexible working time system is agreed, consider appointing a group of employees from across the organisation to help steer the project through and resolve any issues or problems. Include union as well as staff representatives, if one or more trade unions are recognised within the workplace.

6 Check the options for change with the working group

Anticipate problems and risks by asking the project group to evaluate all the accepted options for change, considering such questions as:

- What system will there be for arranging cover?
- Will you allow line managers the right to refuse flexi-leave on work grounds?
- How will you ensure parity of treatment in training and development, promotion and benefits?
- Will the system fit with relevant legislation, such as the Work and Families Act 2006 and the Equalities Act 2010 in the UK?

- Will there be any additional costs, and will these be offset by business benefits?

7 Communicate the policies to all staff

Publicise the flexible working time system widely before it is launched. Show how it will work, giving some illustrative examples. Be open about any terms and conditions of eligibility for each option, and set guidelines for their use.

8 Identify a coordinator

Appoint someone as a coordinator to retain a general overview of the flexible working time scheme as a whole and offer guidance on its implementation.

9 Provide training for managers or team leaders in implementing flexible working hours

To enable managers to ensure that work gets done, some continued management control is vital as flexibility is introduced. If there are areas where flexible working hours cannot be used for business reasons, it is best to agree these centrally to avoid any resentment towards managers who need to make exceptions.

10 Evaluate the scheme

Work out how to monitor and evaluate the success of flexible working, so that you can highlight areas where adaptations may be needed, and measure the expected business benefits.

11 Consider whether changes in culture or attitudes are needed

If people find it hard to adapt to the flexible working environment, you may need to consider supporting the new practices with a planned programme to change attitudes or organisational culture.

As a manager you should avoid:

- gearing flexible working options only towards women with children
- making assumptions about employees' needs and wishes
- ignoring the cover and other problems that some options, such as term-time working, may cause for full-time staff
- overlooking the need to invest more time in scheduling work if the annual working hours approach is taken – be aware that, in practice, this option is hard to control over a long period
- allowing communications between job sharers to break down and create possible continuity problems.

Implementing a diversity management programme

The concept of diversity encompasses any sort of difference between individuals. It covers anything that might affect workplace relationships and achievements, such as ethnic origin, age, disability, gender, sex and sexual orientation, family status, education, social or cultural background, personality or attitudes. The management of diversity involves developing and implementing strategies through which a network of varied individuals are integrated into a dynamic workforce.

Diversity management goes beyond what is required by legislation designed to promote equal opportunities and prevent discrimination. It comprises an approach that recognises and values differences and aims to make positive use of the unique talents and perspectives within the workforce. The focus is on individuals, rather than minority groups.

The increasing globalisation and competitiveness of business together with a growing body of equal opportunities legislation have led to a heightened awareness of and interest in diversity issues. Although all employers have to comply with anti-discrimination legislation, some will be further along their diversity journey than others.

The management of diversity aims to promote an inclusive culture and a positive working environment in which individuals are valued and respected. Managing diversity can contribute to:

- the realisation and development of employees' full potential

- improved employee engagement, motivation and empowerment
- better morale and job satisfaction, leading to greater productivity
- improved employee retention, leading to reduced recruitment and training costs
- an increase in the flow of ideas, leading to greater creativity and innovation
- greater flexibility within the workforce
- the recruitment and promotion of those with the best skills and abilities, leading to competitive advantage
- compliance with the requirements of equal opportunities legislation and the elimination of discriminatory behaviour
- a workforce that is better equipped to serve a diverse customer base and diverse markets, leading to high levels of customer satisfaction
- improved ability to compete in global markets
- enhanced corporate image, as the organisation is seen as a socially responsible employer.

This checklist outlines the principal action points for implementing a diversity management programme.

Action checklist

1 Gain top-level support

Approach directors and managers in your organisation and convince them of the advantages of active diversity management. Present the business and social cases for a diversity initiative, for instance the costs of harassment, retention rates, complaints, grievances and court cases. If necessary, conduct high-level diversity awareness training to develop the commitment of key decision-makers.

2 Assign financial and human resources to the programme

Don't underestimate the time and money that will be needed, and look to the long term – the programme will extend over years rather than months. At this stage, identify as many people as possible who can act as change agents, lead the initiative and cascade it throughout the organisation.

3 Set your goals

Decide what you want the programme to achieve and set your goals accordingly. Methods that can be used to identify diversity management objectives include consultation, brainstorming, benchmarking and literature reviews. Ensure that the goals set are specific and achievable. Possible objectives might be to:

- increase the proportion of women in the workforce to 50%
- enable more flexible working practices, such as more home working
- facilitate recruitment from a wider geographical or cultural area.

Gain the support of employees for these goals, and relate them to the organisation's overall vision and mission statement and any other organisational initiatives.

4 Establish current levels of diversity management

Plan and conduct a diversity audit to gauge existing levels of diversity in your organisation. You will need to assess both qualitative and quantitative evidence, focusing on people, processes and strategies. Find out:

- which kinds of difference affect the ability of individuals to achieve their potential in your organisation
- the extent to which these differences create disadvantages or advantages for employees
- how organisational procedures and strategies affect different groups of employees.

Some data-gathering methods include:

- questionnaires – design these with your target audience in mind and ensure anonymity and privacy for respondents
- individual and group interviews – consider who should conduct these and how to create an informal atmosphere
- focus group discussions – you could, for example, talk to groups of female, disabled, ethnic minority or older employees
- unobtrusive observation – a discreet walkabout can be revealing
- document surveys – examine written procedures, personnel records, customer complaints, publicity material and any other documentary evidence within the organisation
- benchmarking – look at organisations similar to your own for examples of good practice to follow and bad practice to avoid.

5 Conduct a gap analysis

Review the audit results and establish how great a difference there is between your current position and your goals.

6 Identify areas where change is needed

Work out what steps will be needed to achieve your goals. You may need to make changes to:

- processes – for example, revising the recruitment procedure
- working arrangements – for example, introducing flexitime, childcare facilities, time off for family responsibilities, more home working
- attitudes – for example, combating intercultural prejudice and improving intercultural communication
- physical environment – for example, creating better access for disabled workers and customers, revising office layout and providing more communal areas.

7 Write a diversity policy

Use these broad ideas for change, together with your diversity goals, to compile a concise written diversity policy. In the UK all documentation should reflect new terminology set out in the Equality Act 2010.

The policy could include:

- a definition of diversity
- reasons why it is important
- the goals of the diversity management programme
- ways in which the goals will be achieved.

Communicate the policy to employees and stakeholders. Put copies on the staff notice board and company intranet and include it in the staff handbook.

It is only when values and policies become embedded in the day-to-day activities of the organisation that any measure of success can be claimed.

8 Compile a detailed diversity action plan

Define the finer details of the programme, specifying exactly how the planned changes will be brought about. Hold brainstorming sessions to generate ideas for action, and then draw up an implementation plan to coordinate and set a timetable for actions to be taken. Make sure the plan includes regular reviews – decide what should be measured and monitored before the programme starts and make data gathering an ongoing part of the plan.

9 Set the programme in motion

Communicate the plan to employees and put it into action. Appoint programme coordinators and publicise their role, providing employees with a focal point for information and feedback.

10 Monitor and review

Monitor the programme over twelve months, and adjust the plan as necessary. Where problems occur, review the diversity policy and decide whether it should be amended.

11 Establish an ongoing programme

Schedule an ongoing diversity programme for the long term. Allow for the programme to change as the organisation's internal and external circumstances change. Ensure that diversity retains a high profile and work towards its internalisation within the organisation. Diversity management should become a natural part of everyday life.

As a manager you should avoid:

- handling diversity issues insensitively, or in a way that could stir up ill-feeling

- invading employees' privacy

- failing to consult and gain commitment throughout the organisation

- implementing policies and programmes without first communicating them to those involved

- confusing equal opportunities with diversity management

- seeing diversity as merely a question of legal compliance

- falling into an 'us' and 'them' mentality – diversity is about inclusiveness.

Introducing flexible benefits

A flexible benefits scheme (also known as cafeteria benefits) is a structured arrangement of cash and benefits that offers choices to employees, enabling them to meet their personal needs. Schemes typically include a core package of pay, holiday and pension, with additional flexible options to a value designated by the scheme. The more comprehensive schemes may also include voluntary benefits, which are purchased and paid for by employees. Flexible benefits are usually funded by the organisation, and therefore any organisation wishing to introduce them will need to think carefully about their financial viability.

Flexible benefits schemes are structured systems that allow employees to choose the benefits that suit their particular circumstances from a selection provided by their employer. Organisations have introduced such systems as part of a wider move to more flexible working and in recognition of employees' differing wishes and needs at different stages of their lives.

Many employees do not fully recognise the worth of the benefits their employer provides, so the move to a flexible benefits scheme is one way of highlighting the totality of the remuneration package. This may have benefits to the employer through increased employee retention and reduced recruitment costs.

Some of the reported advantages of introducing flexible benefits include:

- staff gain a sense of control

- dual-career couples can choose complementary benefits and avoid duplication
- employers are seen as recognising the diverse needs and different life-stages of their employees
- the provision of benefits becomes less contentious
- employees appreciate the true worth of the benefits package
- improvement in staff retention and attraction of new talent.

This checklist explains the main steps in defining a strategy and in implementing a flexible benefits scheme. Managers are advised to seek advice on the tax implications for both the organisation and the individual.

Action checklist

1 Define the strategy

Before starting to develop your strategy for flexible benefits it is important to determine whether your organisation needs such an approach. Planning and implementing a full flexible benefits scheme will require time and money, so it is important to be clear about your reasons for doing so, especially in times of uncertainty or austerity.

Consider the following:

- What is the market offering for the industry you work in?
- Do you fully understand the context of your existing reward strategy? Does a flexible benefits scheme provide a good fit?
- What is the motivational and financial value of your existing reward package?
- What do you hope to gain by implementing a flexible scheme?
- Have you asked your employees what they like and dislike about your existing approach?
- Could you use a focus group or staff survey to investigate this area?

You might decide that simple changes to your existing package of benefits will meet your objectives. For example, would allowing employees to buy and sell holidays, make additional payments into their pension scheme and use salary sacrifice to buy childcare vouchers provide a simpler route to improving staff perceptions of your benefits package? Would the provision of an annual total rewards statement raise staff awareness of the value of the existing benefits?

If you decide that a flexible scheme provides a good strategic fit, make sure you allow plenty of time to research, plan, implement and communicate with employees.

2 Decide on the form of benefits package

There are a number of issues you need to address. You need to determine:

- whether you will design the scheme in-house or use a consultant
- your policy for providing core benefits
- your mix of core and flexible benefits
- how you plan to administer the scheme
- how employees will select or purchase benefits
- the benefits that are on the menu
- the enrolment process
- the enrolment period for existing employees and for new recruits
- how you will promote the scheme to employees
- how you will evaluate the success of the scheme.

3 Designing and administering the scheme

You can either design and administer the scheme in-house or outsource the process to a specialist company. You may decide on a hybrid approach, whereby you use a consultant to help design the scheme but administer it in-house using your own staff.

The in-house approach requires the allocation of staff time and budget. Also, as most organisations now adopt web-based administration solutions, you need to consider whether you have the technical ability to develop your own scheme or whether you could use one of the many existing programmes. Realistically, the latter may be an option only for small and simple schemes. Many of the computerised systems that are used for administering such schemes include an option that allows employees to model their own choices, which can simplify the process.

You may decide to use a consultant to identify appropriate benefits suppliers. One advantage of this is that they should already have contact with many suppliers and may be better placed to negotiate discounts.

There are a number of consulting organisations that will take on the whole process of design, implementation and administration. Many have their own administration software or work closely with the producers of one of the administration packages. You may benefit from this ability to negotiate good rates for insurance and pensions, and the consultants may be able to add value through their existing relationships with retailers.

Consultants may also be willing to distribute and analyse employee opinion surveys, handle focus groups, design and implement the scheme, and handle the communication process. They will have a wealth of experience from projects with other clients and should be able to save you time in understanding the marketplace and creating solutions to satisfy the diverse requirements of your employees.

It is important to fully understand the cost implications of all these approaches before making a decision.

4 Organise the structure of the scheme

Most schemes stipulate that employees must retain certain core or mandatory benefits. These should take account of tax and employment law requirements, such as the minimum holiday allowance and the provision of staff pensions. Employees may not opt for flexible benefits, for example via salary sacrifice, which take them below the national minimum wage. You may decide that certain staff benefits also make good business sense, such as private medical insurance. Typically, however, organisations try to keep the core element of a scheme to a minimum to give employees as much choice as possible.

5 Decide on the benefits menu

Most flexible schemes are launched with a variation of the existing benefits package, but you may decide to start from scratch or extend the options to provide a far wider range of benefits for selection. The challenge is to provide a menu of benefits which satisfies the needs of all eligible staff, but which does not confuse by providing too much choice. Some of the most common benefits offered are:

- childcare vouchers
- critical illness insurance
- dental insurance
- healthcare cash plans
- holidays
- pensions
- retail vouchers
- travel insurance.

Make sure that your menu is of interest to employees at all stages of their career and with varying personal circumstances.

6 Define the enrolment options

You need to determine a process for enrolling on the scheme and for making changes to selections. Online enrolment via an intranet or secure internet connection may be the only feasible option for large schemes, but you need to consider whether all employees have access to the web during their working day. It may be necessary to make computers available to employees who do not have their own workstation.

Paper-based enrolment may be the only option when few employees have regular online access in the workplace. The documentation should include a personalised preference form, which typically contains details of their current benefit entitlement, the value of the available flex fund and the cost of the different options available. Staff and an administrative process must be in place to handle the returned forms.

Whichever approach you adopt, it is common practice to send a confirmation of the selections, possibly for the individual to sign. You may also need to allow a period of time for reconsideration.

Total reward statements may be distributed at a specified time after the selection process has changed. This serves to remind employees of the value of the total package and also keeps the flex scheme in people's minds. Online systems often produce an indication of total value during the selection process.

Remember also that people's circumstances may change – for example, they may suffer a bereavement – and this may have an effect on the benefits they wish to use. It is advisable to set out the terms of when and how employees can change their benefits.

7 Communicate with employees

Organisations that have adopted flexible benefits have found that effective communication is key to successful employee engagement. Develop a communication strategy that:

- provides an introduction to the plan for all new employees
- drip-feeds information to staff before the launch – via newsletters, for example
- includes a high-profile launch event
- provides a detailed explanation of how the scheme works and the range of choices available
- educates employees about some of the technical tax issues, such as salary sacrifice
- encourages staff enrolment and selection of options

- follows up on employees who do not enrol
- promotes the scheme, once it is up and running, to maintain interest and increase participation
- keeps employees informed of changes to the scheme.

Appropriate communication methods may include:

- road shows and formal presentations
- the corporate intranet
- newsletters, bulletins and posters
- personal letters to employees
- emails
- one-to-one consultations.

Giving a scheme distinctive branding has helped organisations to increase awareness among employees and promote awareness. The name chosen should reinforce the message that the scheme is about giving employees more choice and personal control of the package.

8 Monitor take-up and develop the scheme

The most successful schemes are likely to be those where the benefits on offer are regularly reviewed. A measure of success commonly adopted by organisations is take-up rate. At its most basic level, this records the extent of employee engagement with the scheme, but you should attempt to delve deeper and record the take-up rate for each benefit on offer.

However, if they take these figures at face value, employers may fail to spot employee concerns and may not fully understand the perceived value of benefits with a low take-up, such as childcare vouchers, to those individuals who do opt for them. Consider using focus groups or an employee survey to get a more complete understanding of perceptions.

As a manager you should avoid:

● making schemes too complex

● rushing to implement a scheme without adequate strategic thinking and communication

● failing to take account of legal requirements and changes to those requirements

● considering that this is a one-off process – successful schemes need refreshing on a regular basis.

Email and internet policy

An email and internet policy explains what is considered acceptable or unacceptable use of email and the internet by employees. It makes clear to employees the consequences of any breaches of policy and informs them of any monitoring of their email or internet activities.

Email and internet access are central to modern communications, as is the use of mobile phones and social media. However, the use of such facilities can also be a source of risk for employers. Risks include breaches of security, feared misuse of working time, and inappropriate messages and subject matter. Business experience highlights problems and opportunities, as well as best practice approaches that can be promoted through formal policies. These should make clear the sort of use that is acceptable or otherwise, and ensure that both employee use and employer management of email and internet communications is within the law.

A clearly stated policy will steer people away from potential misuse, abuse or illegal use, and help lessen the possibility of disciplinary action. It can help prevent people from using email to bully or harass others, or accessing unauthorised or illegal sites on the internet. In this way, a policy should reduce the risk of potential claims against an organisation by other employees or external third parties.

Guidance on email etiquette and the internet use allowed might be included in a policy, and enforcement would ultimately rely on normal disciplinary channels. Managers should, however, be aware of the need to detect potential problems and take preventive action before sanctions or penalties become necessary.

Many employees are likely to be using social networking, such as writing a blog or contributing to social networking sites. It would be worthwhile to include some guidance on acceptable use of social networking sites, for example to avoid difficulties when writers identify themselves as members of your organisation and then criticise the organisation, your competitors, or political figures and parties. In practice, it may be difficult to separate workplace and private use of social networking sites, particularly if home or mobile workers access them or your organisation uses them to gain intelligence on competitors.

This checklist aims to help organisations that need to draw up a policy or charter on employees' use of email and the internet. It is not particularly concerned with the procedural aspects of setting up a policy (although procedural aspects are considered), but focuses principally on content.

Action checklist

1 Ensure cross-functional consultation and input

Email and internet policies are often drawn up by information security staff, but an initial cross-departmental task group should include HR personnel, operational and line managers, and any trade union representatives. Where unions are not recognised, employee representatives should be included.

2 Define the terms of reference for the policy

The main focus of this checklist is on email and internet use, but you may also consider including network protection or other areas, as there is a strong overlap between different information and communication technologies and related security issues. Increasingly, organisational policies also cover mobile phones and use of imaging technologies. You will, at the very least, need to consider how your email policy will work in an integrated way with wider IT and security policies.

3 Summarise your organisation's usage policy at the start

Most staff using computers can send and receive external emails and access the internet, although some organisations have opted for a ban on accessing anything other than email. The policy should focus mainly on clarifying what is acceptable within the organisation. Being too inflexible, however, is likely to cause more problems than it solves, and most organisations allow an element of personal use, as long as it does not undermine work or involve illicit messages or sites. A sample statement on broad usage is as follows:

The responsible use of internet and email services to support the organisation's objectives is allowed and encouraged, but should comply with relevant laws and regulations. Users should be aware of IT security and privacy concerns, and should know of and comply with managerial directives on internet usage.

The organisation's internet and email services are resources like any other equipment or facilities the organisation provides, and are to be used only for authorised purposes. The importance of employee ability in using the internet in the interests of the organisation is recognised, and all employees should respect any relevant restrictions on company premises and both during and outside company working time.

4 Set specific restrictions

You need to specify particular limitations that are required.

Organisations need to ensure that employees do not spend excessive time on email or internet use, do not use systems in illegal ways, and do not make personal use of system facilities beyond acceptable, and preferably stated, limits. This may include reasonable use for purposes such as sending and receiving personal email, depending on the general culture of the organisation. Users can be referred to separate or supplementary guidelines giving full details on uses that will constitute bad practice or even misconduct, but it is wise to be explicit about requiring employees not to access sites that are undesirable or inappropriate, and to use filtering software to reinforce this requirement. Examples include online gambling sites, or sites that are indecent, racist or otherwise offensive.

On email, a separate code of etiquette or practice will, ideally, specify requirements relating to politeness, level of acceptable personal use, efficiency, setting up out-of-office messages, requirements for appended disclaimers, use of distribution lists, accurate subject field labels, deletion of messages, respect for privacy and chain letters. The Data Protection Act includes requirements specific to email such as responsibility for disclosure and data.

To comply with legal requirements

Under UK law, employers are generally liable for what employees do in the course of their work, and will be at risk if offensive emails are sent or illegal sites are accessed. It is therefore important to consult the company secretary and/or take legal advice about the laws that apply to email and internet communications and use. These are likely to include areas such as data protection, copyright, contracts, company law, human rights and online defamation. In the UK, for example, the Companies Act 2006 brought in changes that came into effect in January 2007. These restated and built on existing requirements concerning the display of company information on paper documentation, and extended these to cover company websites and email. The requirements include full company name and trading name, details of place of registration, registered office address, registered company number and other information.

To give information on security, retention, deletion and archiving

Information should be included on procedures for scanning or monitoring, blocking of emails or internet site access, system administrators' rights of access, opening and closing of individual computer and email accounts, password creation and updating, authorisation of misuse investigations, virus or spam scanning or auditing, email message storage and lack of total confidentiality. Clarify issues where necessary; for example, most organisations would strictly forbid non-business-related software downloaded from the internet or elsewhere, as it is a potential security risk and could require licensing agreements.

Copyright and plagiarism

Pay particular attention to the downloading and storage of copyright material from the internet. Be clear about, and make clear to employees, the extent to which your organisation is licensed to download, store and reuse material that it has access to (for example, through electronic journal subscriptions). It is desirable that the origin of any such downloaded document is known and preferably attached to the document metadata or otherwise included in the document. This will lessen the risk of infringing intellectual property law or plagiarism. Make it difficult or even impossible to permanently store material owned by third parties in your own corporate archives.

5 Consider implications for home or mobile workers

Employees increasingly access organisational systems from their home or remote locations, and this may introduce further security risks. Equally, if they do internet-related company work on their home computer, their virus protection and software compatibility will need to be checked. Where employees use personal email accounts, consider the level of risk you are prepared to accept if they send files to their own computers, for example. Offering remote access via a secure web-based log-in reduces the risk of corporate information being compromised. It is important that employees understand the extent to which they can identify themselves with the organisation when using social networking sites or blogs. They should be aware of their roles as ambassadors for the organisation; if they have at any time declared their link to your organisation, they must avoid public attacks on the organisation, its suppliers or competitors, or public figures. Further restrictions may be necessary, for example in the public sector, to avoid links to political organisations from employee blogs, websites or posts.

6 Include information on internet and email monitoring

If you are monitoring employees' email communications and internet use you will need to give warning of this. For example:

Incoming and outgoing emails, use of internet facilities and content of attachments may be monitored, and employees should not expect that their use of the company's systems will always be private.

You should ensure that a similar warning to external recipients is included in all emails, either added automatically by your system or as standard wording in all email signatures.

7 Communicate the policy

While a clear, comprehensive and current policy on email and internet use is essential, bringing it to the attention of your employees (and maintaining their awareness of it) is equally important. Managers should be involved in communicating the policy to employees, and can play a strong preventative role by detecting and dealing with problems at an early stage. In unionised organisations, it is likely that employee representatives will have been consulted, and this may support better acceptance of the policy. Regular updating of the policy will help to maintain awareness and appreciation of its importance. It would be useful for employees to acknowledge their understanding of the policy at suitable intervals; this could be done at the same time as reminding employees of your information security and other related policies. The policy can also be included in contracts of employment (for employees), terms of engagement (for contractors) and contracts (for business partners and suppliers). It should also form part of a wider information security policy, which should be formalised and published in areas where staff and visitors can be reminded of its scope and existence.

8 Maintain a watching brief

Fashions in social networking come and go in a matter of months, so you may be devoting energy to writing a policy for something that few people now use – new applications for the web or mobile phones appear frequently, much faster than you can revise the policy. If a new issue appears to be developing it can be useful to ask what people are trying to achieve rather than focusing on the service they are using to do it; for example, if employees air company problems on social networking sites, this could indicate a problem with your grievance procedures.

As a manager you should avoid:

- making a policy too rigid or inflexible – it may be ignored or hinder employees' use of the system
- being vague about what is acceptable and what is not
- failing to check the legal aspects of the policy with a professional adviser.

Handling complaints

A complaint is an expression of lack of satisfaction with a product or service. It may be made verbally or in writing, and may come from an internal or external customer.

The introduction of a complaints handling policy provides a clear approach which will ensure that any complaints received are dealt with courteously and resolved effectively. It can also develop employees' understanding of and confidence in handling complaints. The existence of a procedure to be followed from the moment a complaint is received can help those receiving complaints to avoid personal feelings of 'guilt', which may lead to defensiveness and hinder the resolution of the complaint. This should be part of an overall management policy which recognises that complaints can be turned around and used, both to improve relations with customers or clients and to gather information that will contribute to improvements.

Courtesy, speed and a personal touch are essential elements of a complaints response procedure. A complaining customer who gets all three will usually emerge as a happier customer, and will feel more satisfied with your service and organisation than before the complaint was made. People who feel this way frequently tell others about it.

Important information about customer needs and wishes can be gathered from dealing with complaints and this should be fed into an overall process of continuous improvement for products, services and customer relations.

This checklist outlines a process for handling complaints in organisations whether they are small or large, in manufacturing or services, in the private or public sector.

Action checklist

1 Establish a common approach for handling complaints

The approach adopted must be accepted and put into practice by all employees, from the top to the bottom of the organisation, including those who do not come into direct contact with customers. Ensure that everyone is thinking about customers in the same way. The approach established is primarily the responsibility of senior management and should be embedded in the organisation's culture.

Bear in mind that in highly regulated industries, such as banking, there may be response targets for the acknowledgement, resolution and escalation of complaints that need to be met.

Remember that when customers complain, they like to be:

- aware of who is dealing with the complaint
- listened to and believed
- treated fairly and efficiently
- kept informed of progress
- compensated if compensation is appropriate.

2 Draw up a standard complaints form

This is a valuable tool and should include the following subheadings.

Receipt details:

- date received
- received by
- department/division

Customer details:

- name
- contact details
- identifier, for example account number

Complaint details:

- action (to be) taken
- date completed
- sign-off
- line supervisor.

3 Ensure complaints are assessed correctly

On receipt of a complaint, the recipient should think of it as an opportunity offering a second chance to satisfy the customer, rather than a threat. Employees should:

- be courteous and empathise with the customer
- satisfy themselves that the information is factual
- allow the customer to voice their feelings fully
- listen actively to ensure that the nature of the complaint is clearly understood
- take responsibility for checking what has happened (though without admitting to any liability or fault at this stage).

Subject to appropriate information seeking and establishment of the facts, the recipient, in conjunction with a line manager if necessary, should assess whether the complaint should be considered a major or minor one.

Minor complaints may result from misinterpretations, misunderstandings, errors of detail, or straightforward carelessness. Major complaints may involve a breach of the criminal law or have health and safety or financial implications.

4 Establish ownership and responsibility

Employees should be empowered to take appropriate action if the complaint is clearly justified and falls within their jurisdiction, and can be rectified immediately. If the complaint cannot be resolved by the recipient, details of the customer and complaint should be noted on the form and passed quickly to the relevant person, section, or level of responsibility. The customer should be told that a reply will be given as quickly as possible, and certainly within a stated time limit. The recipient of the complaint should give his or her name – there is nothing more frustrating than dealing with a faceless organisation, or being passed from one person to another.

5 Establish escalation procedures

In the case of major complaints, the manager should decide on the appropriate action. This may involve:

- consulting a higher authority
- the production of a detailed report on the incident
- contact with the organisation's solicitor
- contact with the police.

6 Emphasise customer contact for complaint resolution

When the nature of the complaint has been properly understood, and the facts have been correctly established, the appropriate action should become apparent. If a customer has a genuine grievance, and should perhaps be compensated, this is not the time for negotiating or bartering. The complaint should be resolved as quickly as possible to the customer's satisfaction, and they should be contacted at regular intervals, so that a progress update can be given.

7 Ensure complaint forms are signed off

When the problem has been resolved, and you are sure that the customer is satisfied, the recipient or their superior should sign off the complaints form and forward it for analysis (see point 10).

In cases where no satisfactory solution is available or the customer is making unreasonable demands of the organisation to correct or compensate for the problem, it may be appropriate to:

- inform the customer that expectations exceeded capabilities
- reaffirm what steps can be taken
- state that a report will be passed on to senior management.

8 Decide on internal corrective action

Having dealt with the complaint, decide whether any system, equipment or personnel-related improvement is needed.
Deal with improvements in internal processes or training and development needs as soon as possible after the complaint is resolved.

9 Build in customer satisfaction checks

After an appropriate interval, such as two weeks, contact the customer to confirm that the complaint was resolved to the customer's satisfaction – and to check that the organisation still has a customer.

10 Analyse complaints periodically

All complaints forms should be forwarded to a central address where a manager has responsibility for regularly monitoring the level and nature of complaints. The results of this analysis should be reported to senior management regularly, together with details of any corrective action taken. This will ensure that any underlying issues are identified and can be addressed appropriately.

As a manager you should avoid:

- failing to take responsibility for resolving problems
- neglecting to investigate the root causes
- resorting to compensation rather than resolving the issue
- allowing employees to

- blame the IT system
- say it's not their department
- take complaints personally or defensively
- allocate blame
- let paperwork block a fast response to complaints
- lose customers through being too offhand, slow or impersonal.

Acknowledgements

The Chartered Management Institute (CMI) would like to thank the members of our Subject Matter Experts group for their generous contribution to the development of the management checklists. This panel of over 60 members and fellows of CMI and its sister institute, the Institute of Consulting, draw on their knowledge and expertise to provide feedback on the currency, relevance and practicality of the advice given in the checklists. A full listing of the subject matter experts is available at www.managers.org.uk/policy/subject-matter-experts

This book has been made possible by the work of CMI's staff, in particular Catherine Baker, Piers Cain, Sarah Childs, Michelle Jenkins, Linda Lashbrooke, Robert Orton, Nick Parker, Karen Walsh and not least Mary Wood, the Series Editor. We would also like to thank Stephen Brough and Paul Forty of Profile Books for their support.

The management checklists are based on resources available online at www.managers.org.uk to CMI members to assist them in their work and career development, and to subscribers to the online resource portal ManagementDirect.

Index